Adultery
IN THE
AMERICAN NOVEL

By Donald J. Greiner

The Notebook of Stephen Crane (editor)

Comic Terror: The Novels of John Hawkes

Robert Frost: The Poet and His Critics

American Poets Since World War II: Ammons through Kumin (editor)

American Poets Since World War II: Levertov through Zukofsky (editor)

The Other John Updike: Poems/Short Stories/Prose/Play

John Updike's Novels

Adultery in the American Novel: Updike, James, and Hawthorne

Understanding John Hawkes

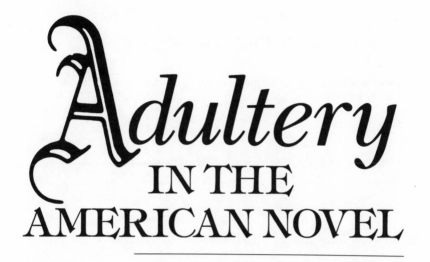

Adultery
IN THE
AMERICAN NOVEL

Updike, James, and Hawthorne

By Donald J. Greiner

University of South Carolina Press

Copyright © University of South Carolina 1985

Published in Columbia, South Carolina, by the University of South Carolina Press

First Edition

Manufactured in the United States of America

Library of Congress Cataloging-in-Publication Data

Greiner, Donald J.
  Adultery in the American novel.

  Includes bibliographies and index.
  1. American fiction—History and criticism.   2. Adultery in literature.   3. Sex in literature.   4. Marriage in literature.   5. Updike, John—Criticism and interpretation.   6. James, Henry, 1843–1916—Criticism and interpretation.   7. Hawthorne, Nathaniel, 1804–1864—Criticism and interpretation.   I. Title.
  PS374.A34G74   1985   813′.009′353   85-14047
  ISBN 0-87249-458-6

As always
this book is
for *Ellen*
And for five boyhood teammates who
became adult friends
Buddy Baker
Al Kirkland
John Orr
Gene Stone
Billy Womack

Contents

Acknowledgments

Acknowledgments are always a pleasure to write. My greatest debts are to Professors John Kimmey and David Cowart of the University of South Carolina for reading the manuscript in progress and for debating the issues with me each step of the way. My graduate assistant, Susan Hayes, cheerfully checked references. Carol Cutsinger did all of the typing. George L. Geckle, chairman, and Chester Bain, dean, provided the released time necessary for research and writing. I am grateful to be a member of the Department of English at the University of South Carolina.

Grateful acknowledgment is made to Alfred A. Knopf, Inc. for permission to quote from the following copyrighted works by John Updike: *Marry Me*; *A Month of Sundays*; *Couples*; *Problems and Other Stories*; *Too Far to Go*; *Rabbit, Run*; *Assorted Prose*; *Picked-Up Pieces*; *Hugging the Shore*; *Olinger Stories*; and *Pigeon Feathers and Other Stories*.

Adultery
IN THE
AMERICAN NOVEL

Updike, James,
Hawthorne, and
Adultery

ohn Updike's current status as a major American author
is largely based on his reputation as a chronicler of
middle-class suburbanites. Arguing that something
fierce goes on in homes, he has avoided topics of apocalypse and extremity to concentrate on the mundane ordinariness of the daily
routine. Man, wife, home, job—these have held his attention since
he published his second novel, *Rabbit, Run*, in 1960. Coming to his
maturity as a novelist in the 1960s and 1970s when the United States
underwent massive social changes that resulted in a realignment of
traditional morality, Updike understood that the new permissive-
ness threatened the cohesiveness of the family. Adultery was one of
the most obvious signs of the shift in moral value. Sexual infidelity
reared its alluring head in public as religious sureties lost their
power to control, and the instability of the family unit mirrored the
general uncertainty of the nation. Little wonder, then, that Updike
became known as *the* author of the contemporary adulterous society.

Yet as Updike realizes, only the emphasis on sexual transgression
has changed. Adultery has been a staple of the novel since the eighteenth century, and the question of who loves whom has intrigued
authors and readers ever since Samuel Richardson sent Pamela
squealing from Squire B., and Henry Fielding persuaded Tom Jones
to learn the lesson of prudence. Updike correctly argues that "the
bourgeois novel is inherently erotic."[1] Rather than bow directly to
the eighteenth century, however, he looks to American fiction, especially as it was shaped by Nathaniel Hawthorne and Henry James.
Where Hawthorne's probing of sexual desire and adultery is framed
by religious and psychological concerns, James's is intertwined with

3

social considerations. Updike unifies both the religious and the social in his novels of adultery. While it may seem a disservice to link him to such giants as Hawthorne and James at this stage of his career, it is clear, as I hope to show in the following chapters, that of all twentieth-century American authors he has synthesized and adapted their tradition. The ambiguity of sexual transgression holds the center of much of their fiction just as it does his.

Thus the purposes of this study are to suggest that Updike is the contemporary inheritor of the Hawthorne-James literary continuum and that a primary subject of mutual concern is adultery. To this end I discuss Updike's numerous secondary comments about his two predecessors in order to establish the frame of reference necessary for a detailed examination of the way he adapts their treatment of transgression. By way of illustration I also offer readings of *The Scarlet Letter*, *The Marble Faun*, and *The Golden Bowl* before turning to Updike's marriage novels.

The Golden Bowl is especially important to this analysis. Like *The Marble Faun*, *Couples*, and *Marry Me*, it investigates a meeting of sexual knowledge and innocence during which the characters hope to turn illicit sexuality into acceptable experience. James's Maggie Verver, however, unlike Hawthorne's Hilda or Updike's transgressors, accommodates adultery and emerges triumphant. One question to pursue in the following chapters is why: Why does James's heroine succeed while Hawthorne's and Updike's equivocate? An answer may be that James dismisses the religious sensibilities that attract the other two authors and stresses a social response to adultery, whereas Hawthorne insists on a moral reaction and Updike an individual one. James's adulterers make mistakes, but Hawthorne's invariably *sin*. The distinction is crucial for Updike because his characters fear that they both err and sin when they sneak toward adultery. What interests me, and what will be discussed later, is that despite these variations on the theme of adultery all three authors show that sexual transgression can lead to creative action. The burden of transgression becomes the triumph of imagination for the novelists and their characters. Such an unexpected equation of creativity and adultery was not possible in American fiction before Hawthorne published *The Scarlet Letter* in 1850.

Updike, James, Hawthorne, and Adultery

I

Sex and transgression have intrigued American authors since William Hill Brown dressed up as fiction a true account of incest among friends of his family and offered *The Power of Sympathy* as the first American novel in 1789. Evidence suggests that *The Power of Sympathy* was suppressed, but five years later, in 1794, Susanna Haswell Rowson published the first American best-selling novel, *Charlotte: A Tale of Truth* (the English edition is 1791). Incest is not an issue for Rowson, but the perils of being seduced and abandoned are, and thus with this feeble spin-off from Samuel Richardson's *Clarissa* Rowson touched the emotions of readers who longed for the passion and tears of sentimental fiction. Titillated by veiled descriptions—often in the pursued heroine's own words—of ungentlemanly behavior and states of undress, the reader could defend his voyeurism with pious claims that he was reading a tale of truth about the lessons of sexual constancy and filial piety. The price of sin, after all, is death, especially if the sin is sexual in nature. Needless to say, Charlotte Temple dies.

Rowson's wretchedly written novel—Leslie Fiedler has wittily remarked that the plot is "almost impossible to retell without improving"[2]—struck a chord among the American populace, and the incredible result is that over two hundred editions of *Charlotte: A Tale of Truth* have been located and described, many of them published in the twentieth century. Never a best-selling novelist like Susanna Rowson, though he tried his best to become one, Charles Brockden Brown added twists of his own to the basic ingredient of sexual misconduct in American fiction. Not content with seduction and abandonment, Brown brings together in *Wieland* (1798) religious mania, voyeurism, murder, suicide, latent incest, a pursued heroine, ventriloquism, and spontaneous combustion of the brain. As ludicrous as the combination may sound to those who have not read the novel, *Wieland* is nevertheless the first American fiction for which serious claims may be made beyond the simple pieties of moral reform. Among other interests *Wieland* introduces the American Gothic hero-villain in Carwin, a man whose haggard face and mysterious past clearly arouse the erotic nature of the suffering

Preliminaries

heroine. Indeed, although Clara is frightened by Carwin's "shaggy locks" and "lustrously black" eyes, she spends the night first sketching and then contemplating his "memorable visage." When the next day dawns, true to Gothic convention, in "darkness and storm" and Clara's bosom "heaves" with sighs, the reader knows that more than fear has been excited.[3] In the short space of one decade, 1789–1798, American fiction was launched with sex as a central focus.

Curiously, however, adultery was not yet an issue. What the prudish Mrs. Wix of James's *What Maisie Knew* (1897) calls "branded by the Bible" had to wait until Hawthorne published the first great American novel in 1850, *The Scarlet Letter*. Before Hawthorne, James Fenimore Cooper had achieved worldwide fame with his Leatherstocking Series, but even in Natty Bumppo's unexplored domain of Indians and nature, sexual desire makes its snakelike entrance. Magua may challenge Uncas for supremacy of the American Eden, and bad Indians may crouch around every bend, but Cora's eroticism is a hidden issue in *The Last of the Mohicans* (1826). The marriage of Cora and Uncas might have solved the problems generated by the confrontation of various bloodlines in the new land, but Magua wants her too. Associated with Milton's Satan, he cannot permit the consummation of the love between Cora and Uncas. More important, neither can Cooper.[4] Fears of miscegenation win the day, and Cooper kills off Cora, Uncas, and Magua, thereby clearing the way for the virginal Alice and the pristine Duncan to become the progenitors of America. The sexually innocent Natty Bumppo merely retreats farther into the forest.

Hawthorne, however, makes explicit what Cooper tries to dodge: that Natty's tract of unadulterated forest land is also the place where the snake crawls into paradise. Natty escapes both apron strings and the sound of the axes when he plunges deeper into the wilderness, but Hester and Dimmesdale enter the forest for another reason. With *The Scarlet Letter* the specter of adultery makes itself known as a primary concern of American fiction. Hawthorne cannot describe the event—the transgression takes place at least nine months before the novel begins—but the opening scene pits the woman taken in adultery against her unforgiving accusers. One cannot help noting the ironic contrast between the rigid Puritans and the compassionate Christ. Confronting a religiously pious but humanly despicable mob, Hester alone knows that both her secret lover and her secret husband are also faces in the crowd.

Full of self-righteous believers, of the kinds of readers who would have required Susanna Rowson and Charles Brockden Brown to pass off their novels as disguised sermons, the accusatory mob screams for everything from Hester's confession to Hester's execution. Their demands to know the name of her fellow adulterer smack of the kind of voyeurism that readers of sentimental fiction indulged in when turning pages in search of the next state of undress. Those few Americans who read novels in 1798 would not have missed the sexual implications in *Wieland* when the desirable Clara grabs a penknife to protect herself from a crazed brother who has murdered his wife in his sister's bedroom. But just as Brockden Brown's readers could have protected their self-respect by claiming to be reading a moral tale that warns against sexual impropriety, so Hawthorne's mob maintains its piety by demanding retribution against a silent adulteress.

Hawthorne himself, however, is no Puritan voyeur, at least not until *The Marble Faun* (1860). Unlike the angry crowd before the scaffold—what Hester calls those iron men and their opinions—he acknowledges the ambiguity of erotic desire. The Puritans may force Hester to cover her breasts with an A and her hair with a cap, but their efforts do little to repress her creative instincts or her voluptuous nature. She is Hawthorne's curious mixture of Madonna with Child and adulteress with bastard, and he refuses to condemn her for sexual transgression as his past ancestors and current neighbors would have done. The unexpected union of Madonna and adulteress personifies Hawthorne's merger of religious sensibility and sexual need, and *The Scarlet Letter* investigates how adultery leads to both creative effort and a stain on the soul.

Such spiritual concerns make Hawthorne seem more Victorian in sexual matters than James. But James has also been persistently misread as the epitome of the prudish novelist even though love and its many entanglements rest at the center of his canon. His symbolism of sexuality is surely as potent as Hawthorne's. From Hester's A through Miriam's catacombs (*The Marble Faun*) to Maggie Verver's bowl is a short way indeed. The difference is that where Hawthorne explores the moral repercussions of adultery, James details the impact of sexual transgression on the social harmony. Because of its complexity, subtlety, and accuracy, *The Golden Bowl* (1904) is *the* American novel of adultery. In it James makes as clear as his sense of fiction will permit that sexual energy both threatens the equilibrium and promises its continuation. Adultery with the predatory Charlotte exposes the crack in the golden bowl, but sex with the newly awakened Maggie covers it up again. James knows that the crack is always there. Not hypocrisy but an admittedly superficial harmony requires that it be repaired if civilized behavior is to be maintained. James learned some of these lessons from Hawthorne. Yet the James-Hawthorne connection, so easily assumed by the general reader and so thoroughly disputed by the informed scholar, has been a bone of contention in American letters since the first reviewers of James's *Hawthorne* cried out against his charge of American provinciality.[5] An overview of their literary relationship is necessary before discussing Updike's place in the continuum because the James-Hawthorne alliance has confused the public eye since James published *Hawthorne* in 1879 and William Dean Howells published "Henry James, Jr." in 1882.[6]

II

Just as James outraged the Americans, so Howells alienated the British. Touting James as the premier contemporary writer of the English language, Howells insisted only James understood that not Dickens and Thackeray but George Eliot and Hawthorne were the precursors of the new realism that James practiced so brilliantly. Sixty years later F. O. Matthiessen agreed in a comment that has since become famous: "James, in a sense, started where Hawthorne left off. . . . His sense of the inadequacy of Hawthorne's loosely finished sketches could again have furnished the stimulus for his reiterated imperative to himself, 'Dramatize, dramatize.'"[7]

James indeed dramatized, but his relationship to Hawthorne remains such a vexing problem that it is not likely to be solved definitively. Perusing the canons of these two great writers, one is always aware of the tension between Hawthorne's defense of Romance, expressed primarily in his prefaces, and James's allegiance to realism, expressed largely in his own prefaces and essays. Hawthorne's so-called national viewpoint—what James mistakenly insisted on as provincialism—is likewise an issue, especially when contrasted with James's international flavor. One does not have to read far in *Hawthorne* before understanding that for James national means parochial while international means cultural. A more important issue, however, is linked to the question of Hawthorne's moral judgment. Although James does not elaborate in his various commentaries on Hawthorne, one understands his sense of Hawthorne's judging his own characters in ways that reflect the New England conscience which shaped his art. Hawthorne may offer alternatives to the characters who are prone to sin, but his stern Puritan morality refuses to let them choose among the possibilities with impunity. Punishment is usually swift and often long. The reader may question the justice of Hester's A, but he is rarely in doubt about the perimeters of Hester's transgression. Updike, for example, follows James and describes Hawthorne's sinners as scrubbing forever at the stains on their souls.

James, on the other hand, refrains from judgment. Closer to Updike than to Hawthorne in this matter, he too offers his characters a variety of alternative actions, but he seldom judges their choices on moral grounds. Like Updike he is more concerned with watching how they adjust to the variables in the ambiguity of the daily routine. Where Hawthorne normally equates transgression with disaster, James sees it in terms of a mistake. Mistakes present his characters with an opportunity for expanded consciousness and thus an invitation to broader experience. For Hawthorne, however, transgression may soil the soul and close the door to life.

The central misdeed in much of their fiction is sexual in nature, even when it is not specifically adulterous, and thus an eye must be kept on their similarities when examining their differences. For example, *The Marble Faun* may be subtitled "The Romance of Monte Beni," and *The Golden Bowl* may be a triumph of realism, but one would be hard pressed to argue that the former lacks the details of realism or that the latter avoids the mysteries of Romance. Miriam's catacombs are as ambiguous as Maggie's pagoda; Hilda's tower is as isolated as Verver's Fawns. Similarly, as Hawthorne suggests the complex association of sexual transgression and punishment by referring to specific paintings, so James hints at the unfathomable mixture of experience and morality by referring to Poe's *The Narrative of Arthur Gordon Pym*. Romance and realism merge to such a degree that one may read *The Golden Bowl* as an extension of *The Marble Faun*. James was surely correct when he denied efforts to differentiate between Romance and novel.

The difference between Hawthorne's moral transgression and James's social wrongdoing is relevant even though James clearly misreads Hawthorne on other matters. If he does not misread, he at least misplaces his emphases in *Hawthorne* so that the earlier author is made to illustrate what the later one wants to believe about America before the Civil War: that its cultural life was so restricted by Puritanism and so warped by prejudice that little serious literature could have been written. The problem is that one cannot be sure whether James equates Hawthorne's so-called isolation with American provincial life or whether he believes the isolation to be the conscious act of a creative genius caught in an unimaginative society. Exaggerating the provinciality of Hawthorne's time, and underplaying Hawthorne's connection with the social milieu, James manages to praise Hawthorne even while he criticizes. The way is thus cleared for his own work to emerge as the first sophisticated American fiction to observe the intricacies of culture. One can only admire James's strategy. What matters, however, are not only his motives but also his views of Hawthorne that he urged on the public in 1879.

James seems amazed at the apparent tranquillity of Hawthorne's career. Representing it as "almost strikingly deficient in incident, in what may be called the dramatic quality," he offers for illustration Hawthorne's notebooks and describes them as "a sort of monument to an unagitated fortune."[8] Stressing that Hawthorne lived most of his life in a small community, he decides that the older writer had little contact with the manners of his day. Still, James calls him "the most valuable example of the American genius," the author to whom most Americans point when they wish to claim to "have enriched the mother-tongue" (2).[9]

When James declares that it takes "a complex social machinery to set a writer in motion," he looks not back to Hawthorne but forward to his own departure from America and resulting fiction of social nuance (3). It is significant that he speaks of an "absence of that quality of realism" and yet suggests that Hawthorne testified to "the sentiments of the society in which he flourished almost as pertinently" as Balzac, Flaubert, and Zola (4). His characters are not

of "actual types" and their speech is not imitative, but his fiction
savors of the society where he has his roots. Even at this early point
in *Hawthorne* the reader can detect James's tendency to take with
one hand what he gives with the other.

A key factor for James and a significant point for this study is
Hawthorne's Puritanism. Picturing Hawthorne's ancestors as not
permitting their resistance of the Indians to weaken "their disposi-
tion to deal with spiritual dangers," James offers a Hawthorne who
was morally "a chip of the old block": "To him as to them, the consciousness of *sin* was the most importunate fact of life" (7, 10). His
ancestors may not have approved of the artist, but they surely would
have honored the man. James looks at Hawthorne and sees the classic Puritan qualities: simplicity, rigidity, firmness, and rationality.
He would have been, says James, on better terms with his grim
forefathers than with his near neighbors: "It is only in a country
where newness and change and brevity of tenure are the common
substance of life, that the fact of one's ancestors having lived for
a hundred and seventy years in a single spot would become an
element of one's morality" (14). As James notes with a condescend-
ing grin, what Hawthorne termed the "moral influence of wealth"
surrounding the successful traders of Salem would not have been
"exerted in the cause of immorality" (16).

James suggests that Hawthorne's solitary nature may have found
its seed in "the social dreariness of a small New England community" in Maine to which Hawthorne moved at age fourteen. Examining Hawthorne's writing, he notes the shades of solitude and finds
"something cold and light and thin, something belonging to the
imagination alone, which indicates a man but little disposed to mul-
tiply his relations, his points of contact, with society" (26). He may
not have been gloomy, but he was not gregarious. Yet if his social
nature did not develop, his imagination expanded to the extent that
James praises the game of hide and seek that Hawthorne played
"among the shadows and substructions, the dark-based pillars and
supports, of our moral nature" (28). Socially isolated and Puritan
bound, Hawthorne developed his penetrating imagination. The
shades and substructions are the light of his art.

This, says James, is "the real charm of Hawthorne's writing—this
purity and spontaneity and naturalness of fancy" (57). James keeps
returning to the quality of Hawthorne's imagination and how it re-

flects the moral nature of "the dusky, overshadowed conscience" (58). Ever the Puritan, Hawthorne had a conscience that was always shaped by "the shadow of the sense of *sin*." Yet here James makes a crucial distinction, one that Updike later confirms. It is not, James writes, that the darkening cloud was a part of Hawthorne's personality but that it was "fixed in the general moral heaven under which he grew up and looked at life" (58). Hawthorne's triumph was that he transferred the burden of morality into the fancy of art. Creating his way clear of the Puritan insistence on retribution, he showed that his sense of sin was not innate but adopted. Thus, says James, his understanding of Puritanism was never theological but always intellectual. His characters are victimized by Puritanism's grimmer aspects, but he himself turned to his imagination to slip through its clutches: "This absence of conviction makes the difference; but the difference is great" (61).

Part of Hawthorne's transcendence through art led him to allegory, which James generally dismisses as "quite one of the lighter exercises of the imagination." Admitting that allegory directs the tales more than the novels, he nevertheless does not approve of such conceits and correspondences, particularly when the idea of the tale is not perfectly united with the ingenious analogies. But in a well-known statement James grudgingly accepts the allegorical trappings in Hawthorne because they define the author's glimpses into the mysteries of soul and conscience: "They are moral, and their interest is moral; they deal with something more than the mere accidents and conventionalities, the surface occurrences of life. The fine thing in Hawthorne is that he cared for the deeper psychology." Defining a Hawthorne who anticipates his own art, James describes the originality of Hawthorne's fiction as his air of "being a confirmed *habitué* of a region of mysteries and subtleties" (65).

Such penetrating glances into the underside of conscience negate Hawthorne's ability to create the social realism that James himself was committed to when he published *Hawthorne*, and thus he writes the line that Updike refers to more than a century later: "Zenobia is, to my sense, his only very definite attempt at the representation of a character" (80).[10] More relevant to James's concern, however, is the eye-catching contrast of Emerson and Hawthorne that has the secondary purpose of criticizing the tranquil cheeriness which James misrepresents as the only acceptable tone of antebellum America: "Emerson, as a sort of spiritual sun-worshipper, could have attached but a moderate value to Hawthorne's cat-like faculty of seeing in the dark" (99). With such power of penetration, James implies, the absence of realism is not of the moment. He understands that when Hawthorne's fancy is keenest, his "dark Puritan tinge" exhibits its richest hues.

Of particular significance to my concerns are James's comments on *The Scarlet Letter* and *The Marble Faun*. Condescension continues to flavor his opinions, but one detects his reluctant admiration for *The Scarlet Letter*: "Densely dark, with a single spot of vivid colour in it; and it will probably long remain the most consistently gloomy of English novels of the first order" (109). Interestingly, he seems to dodge in 1879 the sexual implications that he will detail in 1904 in *The Golden Bowl*. Insisting that Hawthorne is concerned not with Hester's transgression but with the "moral situation" during the intervening years, James—mistakenly it seems to me—argues that Hester becomes an "accessory" figure and that the denouement depends on Dimmesdale. He finds in Hawthorne's novel of adultery a reticence that today's readers surely question: that Hester and Dimmesdale loved each other "too well" was to Hawthorne "of an interest comparatively vulgar" because he saw the novel not as a revelation of passion but as an account of its sequel (112). This emphasis, of course, is generally acceptable, but it permits James to ignore the erotic undertones of the meeting in the forest and the minister's subsequent longing for adolescent girls. Given this peculiar point of view, one understands James's elevation of the passionless Hilda over the sensual Miriam in *The Marble Faun*. The dark woman barely arouses James's interest, but the blond girl is, incredibly, "an admirable invention—one of those things that mark the man of genius" (168). Not mysterious sensuality but inhibited Puritanism strikes James as the true focus of Hawthorne's last novel. What a long way his opinion is from the passion of *The Golden Bowl*. In his summation of Hawthorne's art he reiterates the interplay of imaginative flight and moral persuasion: "He combined in a singular degree the spontaneity of the imagination with a haunting care for moral problems" (183).

This summation is both succinct and fuzzy. One knows what James says, but one is not quite sure where he stands in relation to the subject of *Hawthorne*. It is as if he questions Hawthorne for the

very material that he himself will later adapt. John Carlos Rowe is
direct when he describes *Hawthorne* as a book marked by an "aggressive denial" of the provincial as well as by the "pressing need" it
expresses for James to "find a tradition of which he might be the
proper heir." Rowe correctly notes that *The Portrait of a Lady* is
James's first major effort to translate Hawthorne's Romance into his
own realism. In Hester and Isabel "the destiny of sin is to be recognized in both the self and those others who shaped the central character's social identity."[11] Recognition of one's private flaws creates
public bonds with other lives. As James learned from Hawthorne, so
Maggie Verver will have to realize that her challenge is understanding the balance between the isolated individual and the crowded
community.

James's eccentric portrait in *Hawthorne* exposed a dilemma that
held his interest off and on for the next thirty-five years: the adaptation of another's sensibility. Influence is not so much the issue as
molding material to one's needs, but in the 1870s James clearly
lacked the confidence to accept Hawthorne when he glanced over
his shoulder at the one American author whose fascination with the
"deeper psychology" sparked his own. Thus, beginning with his
1872 review of Hawthorne's *French and Italian Notebooks* (*Nation*,
14 March 1872) and with the 1879 *Hawthorne*, James continued
to rethink, reevaluate, and revise his understanding of the necessity for that backward glance. His 1897 essay on Hawthorne for
Charles Dudley Warner's *Library of the World's Best Literature* and
his 10 June 1904 letter to Robert S. Rantoul for the Hawthorne centennial look not only back to *Hawthorne* but also forward to his final
formal remarks about his predecessor in *Notes of a Son and Brother*
(1914). As Peter Buitenhuis has shown, James toned down his earlier
critical view to the extent that the 1904 letter confesses a sympathy
bordering on nostalgia.[12] Rather than cry out against Hawthorne's
separation from culture, James now argues that some measure of
alienation was necessary for Hawthorne to write his observations of
American sensibility with detachment. If in 1879 Hawthorne is a
provincial allegorist preoccupied with Puritan consciousness, in
1904 he is a nostalgic reminder to the aging James of a lost, sim-
pler time.

One feels the temptation to point to James's change of opinion as a
sign of maturity, but one resists. Motive is still an issue. Redefining

the impact of his literary ancestor, he reeducates the reader to accept Hawthorne as preceding him in the courageous decision to isolate himself from his native society for the benefit of art. His later accounts of the adaptation of sensibility indicate not only development but also desire to create different views of Hawthorne according to his requirements at the time. As Rowe correctly says about *Hawthorne*: "James mythologized Hawthorne as the last American innocent, alienated by the provinciality of young America, precisely to establish a local and native American tradition that James would hazard to take up in order to denationalize. . . . An international James, free from the boundaries he invents to trap his Hawthorne, might escape to overtake that very ambiguous figure which Hawthorne continued to cut for James from 1872 to 1914."[13]

No one, including James, denies the example of Hawthorne as the first American author who showed him how the deeper psychology could be transformed by the imagination into art. Conscious of Hawthorne's ability to penetrate, James united Hawthorne's tendency to probe with his own commitment to observe. The result is a kind of architectural marvel: the inclusion of a Gothic attic in a Victorian drawing room. But once that is admitted, James must slay the father, and this he does by emphasizing not the benefit of New England society but the limitation of national consciousness. James has to stress what to his mind are Hawthorne's defects in order to imply his own success in solving Hawthorne's problems. In short, Romance must be undercut to validate realism. To make his point James even suggests that his forerunner realized the flaws in Romance and attempted to step toward psychological realism with the characters of Coverdale and Zenobia in *The Blithedale Romance*. Isolating Hawthorne in this peculiar perspective, he can then put forward his own achievement as fulfilling Hawthorne's promise.

Efforts to separate fiction into the poles of the Romance and the novel continued to interest James. Two of his essays—"The Art of Fiction" (1884) and the preface to *The American* (volume 2 of the New York Edition)—are especially relevant, and while they are not specifically about Hawthorne, they do illustrate his hesitation to endorse the separation of Romance and novel. One wonders whether "The Art of Fiction" is not an indirect response to Hawthorne's attempt to differentiate his own kind of writing, for the essay exemplifies James's expansive vision, his generous sense of the total art

Preliminaries

of fiction. Not prescription but imagination is his advice to the aspiring writer: "Try to be one of the people on whom nothing is lost!"[14] Such a novelist, suggests James, understands that the two primary obligations of fiction are that it represents life and that it is interesting. Moral concerns, as they are filtered through religious inhibitions or notions of sin, have little to do with the novel. Note that James singles out Protestantism: "'Art,' in our Protestant communities, where so many things have got so strangely twisted about, is supposed in certain circles to have some vaguely injurious effect upon those who make it an important consideration. . . . It is assumed to be opposed in some mysterious manner to morality, to amusement, to instruction."[15]

James has in mind, of course, the Puritan division of fiction and truth that plagued Charles Brockden Brown, but he counters charges of immorality by arguing that a good novel—good in all senses of the word—is that which possesses "the sense of reality." By "reality" he means not the truth of fact that the Puritans called for but the "solidity of specification." Moral values follow the author's skill in communicating an air of reality. (Interestingly, Updike will later join James and insist that moral fiction is accurate fiction, and yet join Hawthorne and subtitle one of his marriage novels—*Marry Me*—"A Romance.") Given James's liberal sense of the novel, one understands why he refuses to follow Hawthorne in distinguishing between the novel and the Romance. On the one hand he furthers the claims of the new realism with his emphasis on fiction that has "life," and on the other hand he reduces the claims of the old definitions with his insistence on fiction that is all-encompassing: "There are bad novels and good novels . . . that is the only distinction in which I see any meaning. . . . The novel and the romance, the novel of incident and that of character—these clumsy separations appear to me to have been made by critics and readers for their own convenience."[16] Since the standard for romancer and novelist is equally high, one may as well call both novelists. Not the kind of material the author uses but what he makes of the material is the primary basis for evaluation: "The essence of moral energy is to survey the whole field." One suspects that, allowing for the difference between social conventions, James would not be appalled by the treatment of adultery in contemporary fiction so long as the province of the novel continues to be "all life, all feeling, all observation, all vision."[17]

More than two decades later, in the preface to *The American*, James developed his ideas about the novel and the Romance that were originally sparked by his reading of Hawthorne. Once again he points to the fallacy of the differentiation: "It is as difficult . . . to trace the dividing-line between the real and the romantic as to plant a milestone between north and south."[18] Devoting a third of his preface to the question of Romance versus novel, he decides that "we must reserve vague labels for artless mixtures." Insofar as one piece of fiction suggests an air of Romance while another communicates an element of reality, James is willing to extend his general appreciation of fiction only to the point that the real represents experience which the reader naturally knows, while the Romance illustrates experience which the reader knows indirectly. Dimmesdale may or may not have an A on his chest in the final scaffold scene, but the possibility is no stranger than that of the Bloomsbury shopkeeper recognizing the photographs of Charlotte and the Prince after he sells the golden bowl to Maggie.

James names *Madame Bovary* as a realistic novel with a romantic temper, and he would surely include *The Golden Bowl* as well. Again he differs with Hawthorne and stresses not the fabulousness of the material but what the author does with his donnée:

> The only *general* attribute of projected romance that I can see, the only one that fits all its cases, is the fact of the kind of experience with which it deals—experience liberated, so to speak; experience disengaged, disembroiled, disencumbered, exempt from the conditions that we usually know to attach to it . . . and operating in a medium which relieves it . . . of the inconvenience of a *related*, a measurable state, a state subject to all our vulgar communities.[19]

Execution is the key. The trick is not to cut the ties to community too rashly. Indeed, says James, the novelist who deals with unusual experience will do well to create the illusion that no sacrifice of the mundane has been made at all: "The art of the romancer is, 'for the fun of it,' insidiously to cut the cable, to cut it without our detecting him." The careful reader understands the way things happen, but the art of fiction is "drugging" the reader so that "the way things don't happen may be artfully made to pass for the way things do." [20] One suspects that James, however grudgingly, would accord Hawthorne this honor.

Thus the author of *The Scarlet Letter* and *The Marble Faun* remained both an artistic father and a prominent adversary for James. Robert Emmet Long's metaphor is apt: "Hawthorne was like a tar baby, from which, once touched, James could never completely free himself." [21] Tar babies and struggle, homage and repudiation—such are the idiosyncrasies of their relationship. Given the complexity of the connection, all James can do in *Hawthorne* is resort to his curious mixture of reluctant praise and eager condescension: "Poor Hawthorne" picked blueberries at Bowdoin College while thousands of miles away scholars flocked through Oxford and Cambridge.

One does not read *Hawthorne* for long before noting that what James finds admirable in Hawthorne he hopes to find admirable in himself. Artistic bias shapes literary criticism. The Hawthornian spectator with a moral interest in life's mysteries and subtleties was bound to appeal to James's developing sense of the possibilities for fiction. The insecurity of condescension is missing from his 1897 essay on Hawthorne, but by that late date, of course, James's achievement in the novel was so secure that he no longer had to challenge the man at the top. Significantly, then, when he published *Notes of a Son and Brother* in 1914, he celebrated Hawthorne for the very quality that he makes Maggie accept in *The Golden Bowl*: the courage to peer behind the exterior veils. Maggie must finally face the adultery and stare at the "thing hideously behind"; but Hawthorne, admits James, knew all along the "quaintness or the weirdness, the interest *behind* the interest, of things." From the advantage of hindsight one understands how *The Golden Bowl* is a moral fable that Hawthorne himself would have appreciated. Maggie's bowl glitters and burns with Hester's A.

No wonder James confesses that he cried when learning of Hawthorne's death. He was twenty-one years old when the giant fell, and he must have conceded that the footprints loomed awfully large. *Hawthorne* may be a troublesome book, yet in the larger sense the problem is not so much James's apparent deception but the evidence of his struggle in coming to terms with the one American author whose sensibility he had to adapt.

III

Hawthorne's Hester and Miriam are denied the qualified happiness that James's Maggie earns through manipulation and experience, and the difference results in part from the contrast between Hawthorne's moral concerns and James's social interests. John Updike combines the two. His spiritually terrified adulterer recognizes the collapse of the social fabric in the post-pill paradise, but he also worries about being drawn back to the apron strings because he fears that fidelity threatens the integrity of his sense of self. Unlike Hawthorne and James, Updike places his adulterer in a paradoxical dilemma that is the result of a religious believer's insisting on the value of his individuality in what one Updike character calls "the twilight of the old morality." Freed in the late twentieth century from the constrictions of a socially agreed-on set of conventions, but longing for the peace that ceremonial and contractural obligations allow, Updike's adulterer finds himself pursuing the self-definition that transgression invites while looking over his shoulder at the security that constancy promises. He knows that according to the dictates of his religion adultery is a sin and thus a threat to his soul, but he also believes that fidelity cuts off his freedom and is thus a threat to his life. Both social harmony and moral surety seem impossible if the transgression persists, but neither force is strong enough in Updike's world to provide definition of right and proper action. No wonder the adulterer in *Marry Me* (1976) imagines three separate endings to his predicament. His inability to choose between wife and mistress, and his realization that social and religious dictates will not decide the matter for him, suggest how different Updike's society is from those of Hawthorne and James.

Another primary difference is that Updike's fictional adulteries are nearly always public. Hawthorne's transgressors agonize in private, their secret sins unrevealed and unrelieved. James's transgressors also keep quiet, yet they do so not for moral reasons but for preservation of the social harmony. Updike's, on the other hand, discuss the adulteries not only with their spouses but often with the spouses of their mistresses. Public confirmation of one's guilt acknowledges the individuality of one's acts. Husbands, wives, ministers, and neighbors all know. Such was not always the case.

Preliminaries

The cult of privacy was jealously guarded in the nineteenth century, and the result was that private motives could hide behind public masks. As Peter Gay notes, "Nearly all cultures, we know, draw some line, more or less distinct, between the personal and public spheres. But nineteenth-century middle-class culture was particularly emphatic about this, making the gulf between private and public as wide as it could manage."[22] In Hester Prynne's case the gulf is so wide that her private exercise of speculation and intellect would have enraged her accusers even more than her adultery had they only known about it. She counters the public humiliation of adultery with the private creativity of art. But Dimmesdale—and Hilda and Miriam—are not so sure of their private selves, and thus the nineteenth-century emphasis on immaculate public behavior requires them to repress guilt to the point of self-laceration and pain. Maggie Verver is closer to Hester and Miriam than to Dimmesdale and Hilda, for she recognizes the need to work through public humiliation by calling on the resources of the self. The mores of her husband will not tolerate scandal, though he is the one guilty of adultery. Accepting the cultural mandate to avoid public exposure of private affairs, Maggie discreetly manipulates all concerned so that her private pressure on the secret transgressors results in Charlotte's public agony. Maggie's private pain from being betrayed becomes Charlotte's public suffering from being discarded. Gay's description of the nineteenth century is apt: "individualistic, introspective, and reticent." The adulterers do not discuss their transgressions, for to do so would be to confess the guilt to all who will listen. Charlotte's sense of being shackled to Adam Verver's leash is not that far from Dimmesdale's voyeurism of his own soul. Neither can publicly admit the cause of the hurt.

Gay writes, "There were, in the nineteenth century as at other times, wishes and fears so stirring or so frightening that one could not acknowledge them even to oneself, and they reached consciousness only by the detour of dreams or slips of the tongue."[23] Updike's late twentieth century is not one of those times. As Gay notes when discussing the prominent role of diaries in the nineteenth century, there was no conspiracy of silence but there was "circumspection, especially about the things that mattered."[24] The thing that mattered most, of course, was sex. Delicacy in all matters physical was the rule of thumb for what Gay calls the "princes of prudence." Committed not so much to a conspiracy of silence as to circumspection about their various falls from grace via the body, the characters of Hawthorne and James resort to reticence while their authors rely on symbol. There is a direct correlation between Hester's and Miriam's and Maggie's refusals to discuss the erotic atmospheres in which they live and Hawthorne's and James's deflection of explicit description into symbolic expression. Hester's letting down her hair is as much a sexual gesture as Maggie's visions of flashing swords, but the appropriateness of the literal level protects the reader who fears being tainted by explicitness. Gay offers the following comment by Hawthorne, who was responding to the receipt of a love letter from his fiancée, Sophia Peabody: "I always feel as if your letters were too sacred to be read in the midst of people—and (you will smile) I never read them without first washing my hands!"[25] Sophia might not have smiled, but today's reader surely does when he compares the chasteness of Hawthorne's sentiments with the eroticism of Hawthorne's fiction. Adultery could be a subject only for novels, and then only if the passion were hidden behind layers of symbolic meaning. It is not that sexual desire was denied but that it was transformed into art. Adultery becomes creative; the religious sensibilities that move the repressed Dimmesdale and Hilda (not to mention Updike's male adulterers) are often another mask for passionate needs. Gay describes an aspiring clergyman in the nineteenth century who was trying to break through his beloved's reserve: "He attempted to coax her into erotic freedom by resorting to socially acceptable religious language as a cloak for his amorous desires."[26] Certain needs are too "holy" to mention. One recalls the adulterous Dimmesdale returning from the forest to write the Election Day Sermon while nearly crazed by blasphemy and lust.

Gay shows that while Hawthorne could not "gush out" his private feelings in the presence of his immediate family, he could express his physical yearnings to Sophia even before they were married: "His erotic imagination was kindled by the frustrations that the bourgeois rules of the courting game inflicted on him, but he did not hesitate to tell her so."[27] Sophia responded wholeheartedly, "evidently," reports Gay, permitting herself and her fiancé "erotic liberties" just short of consummation. Her later censoring of her husband's diaries was not the act of a sexually repressed woman but the response of a Victorian lady bowing to the prevailing boundary between private action and public exposure. Reticent expression did not always mean inhibited desire. Lawful passion within marriage was the key.

But Hawthorne and James rarely wrote about lawful sexuality publicly consecrated by religious ceremony and judicial contract. The threat of adultery or transgression itself hovers at the center of their fiction as each author investigates how free sexual expression affects either moral or social stability. The divorce trials that rocked London in the mid-1880s, which I will discuss later, would have shocked Hawthorne as much as they disturbed James, for public revelation of private indiscretion violated the propriety of silence about all things physical. In this sense, then, adultery is not only transgression but also revelation of the inner life, of what James described in Hawthorne as the "deeper psychology." Although Hawthorne is more concerned with religious nuance than James, *The Marble Faun* is the ancestor of *The Golden Bowl* in its discussion of the intermingling of sexuality and art. Creativity and morality are involved in both the erotic and the artistic, as Hawthorne and James—and Updike—well knew. Writing of James's book *Hawthorne*, Edmund Wilson observes that James "was to revert in *The Golden Bowl*, his last completed novel, to a symbolism that goes straight back to Hawthorne. . . . And there is also the moral preoccupation, the refinement of the Puritan conscience, of which Hawthorne had been the great exemplar and which was to continue to motivate James through the whole of his literary career." [28]

Updike belongs in the Hawthorne-James continuum. It is not so much a matter of what Harold Bloom terms "the anxiety of influence" as it is the adaptation of a sensibility. Sex, guilt, and belief are issues vital to the three authors in varying degrees, but adultery is commonly the touchstone. With his explicit references to Hawthorne in *A Month of Sundays* (1975) and his veiled allusions in *Marry Me* and *Couples* (1968), Updike nods to the author of *The Scarlet Letter* and *The Marble Faun*. Yet the many references to James in Updike's essays and reviews suggest that the author of *The Golden Bowl* is equally a major factor in Updike's literary heritage. Much is to be gained by examining Updike in terms of an earlier American tradition that he shapes to his own needs. His culture is as public as those of Hawthorne and James were private, so much so that transgression is discussed not only by the interested neighbors but also by the guilty adulterers. One cannot imagine an Updikean adulterer following the examples of Hester and Maggie and keeping silent about his erotic adventures. But one can imagine the private agony that sears the major characters of all three novelists when the snake oozes its way into the garden.

That famous reptile is just the point. Hawthorne, James, and Updike explore the necessary contrasts between the prelapsarian paradise and the post-Edenic world. Adultery is an issue, for transgression represents the snake itself as it sneaks into Hawthorne's forest, James's drawing room, and Updike's suburb. Hawthorne and Updike are more religious writers than James, more thoroughly Puritan-haunted, and this may be why Updike has assimilated Hawthorne a bit more formally than James. But the fact remains that for all three novelists adultery is a bridge between the garden and the world. Moral implications are always present, either directly in Hawthorne and Updike or peripherally in James.

William Shurr has observed that until "yesterday" America was a religious culture. Discussing the "particular variety of Christianity"—Calvinism—that insists on the domination of Satan and the resurrection of the elect, Shurr notes the disturbing role of women in fiction which, like Hawthorne's "Rappaccini's Daughter," reflects the Calvinist tradition in American letters: "In this world sexual love does not lead to marriage and consummation but to the convulsive death of the seductive woman." He has in mind Beatrice Rappaccini, whose power is "girdled tensely . . . by her virgin zone."[29] Sex and guilt meet in a Calvinist atmosphere, and ˇone understands Shurr's point that this peculiar form of religion is an unusual expression of Christianity in which "the probabilities are in favor of Satan." Shurr focuses on the Calvinist heritage in American literature, while I discuss how Updike adapts the union of religion, sexual transgression, and spiritual or social contract to his own art in his own time. The convulsive death of the seductive woman is not a primary question in Updike's fiction or in that of the other author he pays homage to, James; but expulsion of the transgressor is another matter altogether. Banishment from the ideal garden to the actual world may be viewed as a death of sorts, but it is more a death of innocence than a loss of life. Myth and literature show that full hu-

manity is realized outside the garden. The prelapsarian state is antithetical to the richly lived life. As Shurr writes, "In a sense we are
all Rappaccini's children and must deal with this heritage as we
can."[30] But another kind of expulsion is an issue in the novels of
James and Updike, where the Calvinist tradition is not the over-
whelming force that it is in Hawthorne and where the transgression,
usually sexual in nature as it is also in Hawthorne, upsets the social
or individual rather than the religious bond. Banishment of the
transgressor is necessary in these cases too, not as a metaphor of
convulsive death but as a means of readjusting the equilibrium.

Where the equilibrium is moral for Hawthorne, it is primarily social for James and individual for Updike. Fiction normally reflects
the culture of its respective era, and the progression from *The Scarlet Letter* through *The Golden Bowl* to Updike's marriage novels illustrates the decline of religious sensibility and social propriety in
the United States. Zenobia's death and Hester's and Miriam's banishment suggest the literal possibility of damnation that will devour all
who violate the boundaries of sexual orthodoxy. But Hawthorne's
culture was more religious than James's. Writing at the tail end of
the Victorian Age and long after religious enthusiasm had swept
America in the first half of the nineteenth century, James also expels
his woman taken in adultery—Charlotte Stant—but he does not
consider damnation to be an issue. With moral bonds weakened, social ties must stand firm, and thus he concentrates on Maggie Verver, the woman who will put the society shattered by adultery back
together without betraying the private transgression to public scrutiny. By the time of Updike religious tenets and social propriety are
former sureties nostalgically to be yearned for. He notes in an interview that Puritanism is "obviously a strain that has contributed
enormously to the make-up of the American identity," and that "not
all of the fading of religious belief" has removed the association of
Puritanism and America.[31] Similarly, in a short essay on *Winesburg,
Ohio*, he comments that as early as 1919 society scarcely existed in
"its legal and affective bonds" for Sherwood Anderson.[32] Although
Updike's Piet Hanema, Tom Marshfield, Jerry Conant, and Rabbit
Angstrom fear for the loss of their souls and the breakup of their
social identities when they hop from bed to bed, they worry most of
all about themselves. The pressures of late-twentieth-century life

are such that the individual has only himself to rely on, and Updike's irony is that adultery both places the transgressor in touch with eternity and threatens him with the dead end of guilt. From Hawthorne's religious concerns to James's social harmony to Updike's individual angst seems a long way. For all three authors, however, adultery is both promise and pain.

NOTES

1. John Updike, "If at First You Do Succeed, Try, Try Again," *Picked-Up Pieces* (New York: Knopf, 1975) 402. See also Jerome Klinkowitz, "John Updike Since *Midpoint*," *The Practice of Fiction in America* (Ames: Iowa State University Press, 1980).

2. Leslie Fiedler, *Love and Death in the American Novel* (Cleveland: World, 1964) 68.

3. Charles Brockden Brown, *Wieland, Three Early American Novels*, ed. William S. Kable (Columbus, Ohio: Charles E. Merrill, 1970) 234–35.

4. See Fiedler for a discussion of this issue.

5. The interested reader may consult Elizabeth Stuart Phelps's pointedly titled article "The Man Without a Country" (1880) for a contemporary reaction against James's audacity, or he may examine John Carlos Rowe's essay (1983) for the latest overview of the disagreement. Phelps, "The Man Without a Country," *The Independent* 26 Feb. 1880; Rowe, "What the Thunder Said: James's *Hawthorne* and the American Anxiety of Influence: A Centennial Essay," *Henry James Review* 4 (Winter 1983).

6. William Dean Howells, "Henry James, Jr.," *Century Magazine* (Nov. 1882): 24–29.

7. F. O. Matthiessen, *American Renaissance: Art and Expression in the Age of Emerson and Whitman* (New York: Oxford University Press, 1941) 301.

8. Henry James, *Hawthorne* (1879; New York: AMS Press, 1968) 1. Hereafter cited parenthetically.

9. See Robert Emmet Long, *The Great Succession: Henry James and the Legacy of Hawthorne* (Pittsburgh: University of Pittsburgh Press, 1979) 158–71 for a summation of Hawthorne's influence on specific Jamesian characters, scenes, and situations. The following comment is relevant: "Again and again James attempts to disavow the native tradition of Hawthorne; and again and again he is drawn back to it" (170).

10. Sarah B. Daugherty suggests that James's dislike of Hawthorne's

Preliminaries

heroines may have been the result of his contrasting them with George Sand's vastly more liberated and passionate women. She believes, however, that in general Hawthorne affected James far more than did Sand. See *The Literary Criticism of Henry James* (Athens: Ohio University Press, 1982) 96.

11. Rowe 82, 83. In general Rowe is concerned with what *Hawthorne* says about "American nationality" and with how later scholars of American literature have used James's discussion of Hawthorne for their own critical theories.

12. Peter Buitenhuis, "Henry James on Hawthorne," *New England Quarterly* 32 (1959): 207–25.

13. Rowe 112.

14. Henry James, "The Art of Fiction," *The Great Critics*, ed. James Harry Smith and Edd Winfield Parks, 3rd ed. (New York: Norton, 1951) 659.

15. James, "The Art of Fiction" 655.

16. James, "The Art of Fiction" 661, 662.

17. James, "The Art of Fiction" 664.

18. Henry James, preface to *The American*, *The Art of the Novel*, ed. R. P. Blackmur (New York: Scribner's, 1962) 37.

19. James, Preface to *The American* 33.

20. James, Preface to *The American* 34.

21. Long 67.

22. Peter Gay, *The Bourgeois Experience: Victoria to Freud* (New York: Oxford University Press, 1984) 1:446.

23. Gay 448–49.

24. Gay 452.

25. Gay 452.

26. Gay 454.

27. Gay 456.

28. *The Shock of Recognition*, ed. Edmund Wilson (New York: Modern Library, 1955) 426.

29. William H. Shurr, *Rappaccini's Children: American Writers in a Calvinist World* (Lexington: University Press of Kentucky, 1981) 2.

30. Shurr 4.

31. William Findlay, "Interview with John Updike," *Cencrastus* 15 (New Year 1984): 31.

32. John Updike, "Twisted Apples," *Harper's* (Mar. 1984): 96.

Part One **The Authors**

Updike and James   1

In March 1974, while giving a speech in Adelaide, South Australia, entitled "Why Write?" John Updike cited Henry James as the benchmark for novelists who aspire to greatness: *"To remain interested*—of American novelists, only Henry James continued in old age to advance his art; most, indeed, wrote their best novels first, or virtually first."[1] The problem, Updike suggests, is not that writers lose their genius but that they confuse the role of the artist with the pose of the great man. Naming Sartre and Faulkner as examples, he points to how a "well-intentioned garrulity replaces the specific witness that has been theirs to give."[2]

Updike's high opinion of James may surprise those who are familiar with his essays on Melville and Hawthorne, for there, and especially in his remarks about the latter, he calls attention to the achievements of two of his great forerunners.[3] The echoes of Hawthorne in *A Month of Sundays* and *Marry Me: A Romance* testify to his awareness of Hawthorne's mastery. Updike's bow to James is not so well known because he has scattered his remarks throughout his nonfiction prose. And yet for more than twenty-five years he has designated James whenever a comparison with the highest standard was called for. His commentary is couched in such a way as to invite discussion of how he and James handle similar interests in realistic depiction of domestic detail, portrayal of character, and the role of adultery in the daily affairs that comprise the social contract.

Updike's continuing celebration of James begins with his sense that James never faltered in pursuit of his goal to become the consummate artist. Advancing his art to the stage where his last three novels are the high point of a long career, James avoided both garrulity and the lure of the public pose. The lesson of the master became a figure in the carpet for Updike. It is a question not of specific influence but of acknowledging the ideal that James represents. As

Updike continues his pace of publishing virtually a book a year since 1958, he is aware of the contrast between James's career and that of America's other great novelist, Faulkner. Faulkner wrote his best novels relatively early and then slipped from the heights of artistic eminence. Although he lived until 1962, his last great novel—*Go Down, Moses*—was published twenty years earlier. James, on the other hand, carefully prepared himself for his finest work, completed his so-called major phase in an astonishing three-year period near the end of his career, and published his most probing book, *The Golden Bowl*, as his last novel. Citing James as the supreme example of continuing achievement in American fiction, Updike admits that the challenge to remain interested nags at him too: "To become less and transmit more, to replenish energy with wisdom— some such hope, at this more than mid-point of my life, is the reason why I write."[4]

But how does an author who aspires to great fiction avoid stumbling into the lair of the great-man syndrome when his likeness is advertised on the cover of *Time* magazine and his presence is required on the Dick Cavett Show? Updike knows the peculiar paradox that plagues American writers: their need of applause and their desire for privacy. Even James, he suggests, felt the opposing tugs: "We are surprised to discover, for instance, that Henry James hoped to make lots of money. . . . The artist's personality has an awkward ambivalence: he is a cave dweller who yet hopes to be pursued into his cave."[5] The question that Updike indirectly asks is how far should he go to avoid the pursuit. The answer, he implies, is to keep writing, as James did.

Such a comparison between Updike and James is not a call for value judgment. *The Gólden Bowl* is eminently more complex than any novel Updike has published thus far. The charge is, rather, to explore how two major novelists, writing a century apart but renowned in their eras for their dissection of adultery and domestic particulars, treat basically the same material. Updike is indeed conscious of how his great predecessor used marriage, sexual transgression, and the complexities of the family contract as metaphors for a society ill at ease with itself. James may chronicle the rich while Updike lovingly inventories the trappings of the middle class, but both authors investigate a social center that may not hold. James, for example, believes that the relationships between lovers can be defined, constantly adjusted, and kept current by maintaining a compromise between social grace and moral value (the Prince returns to Maggie and is grateful). Updike, on the other hand, shows a society constantly breaking down because moral value is relative and social grace a mask for domestic duplicity (the narrator in "Solitaire" chooses wife or mistress, duty or desire, according to the turn of a card). Thus while James responds to adultery from a social perspective, Updike insists on an individual reaction that is denied the traditional sureties of social pressure and moral precept. An examination of Updike's numerous secondary comments about James will establish the framework necessary for a discussion of their literary relationship.

I

Living in London in 1969, Updike was aware of James as a hovering ghost likely to confront any American author posing as a chronicler of English domestic manners. In an essay written for *The Listener* (January 1969), "Notes of a Temporary Resident," he muses that no American can ever truly gain entry to the innermost rooms of English society. The languages may be similar, but the nuances are an ocean apart. Even James, writes Updike, is not the Anglicized American but the American observer of Anglicans: "In the end, there are recesses of England that exist only for initiates. . . . Some Duchess, if memory serves, said at the funeral of our greatest Anglophile, Henry James: 'Poor Mr. James. He never quite met the right people.'"[6] James might not have agreed with the mourning Duchess (after all, he dined with the Prime Minister), but her point—and Updike's—is worth noting. James cultivated the right people in his role as long-boarding guest who watched from a certain distance the intrigues of those all but inaccessible social recesses. Updike, by contrast, seems to have walked out of the various American suburbs where he has lived in order to tell the tale. In both cases the ambiguous nuances of the social whirl inform the centers of their fiction. James's stories of American entries into the English upper class may be long, observes Updike, "but really a novel, even a quite bulky one—you think of Henry James's eight hundred pages—has only a few hinges."[7]

This sense of James as the ultimate artistic standard informs the most significant part of Updike's nonfiction prose, the essay-reviews in which he sets down his thoughts about novels, novelists, and the general state of fiction. Always insisting on his status as an amateur commentator, he nevertheless keeps his opinions before the public. His tone is often that of informing his readers while educating himself. And yet other than the sheer variety of the material he chooses to review, a notable factor is the presence of James. A reading of Updike's large collections of essay-reviews suggests that James is in the background when Updike writes about contemporary fiction. It is not a matter of a novice kneeling at the pedestal of the master but of acknowledging the standards James set for himself when insisting on the importance of the artist and refining the quality of his prose.

Obviously a writer need not think or write like James, but for Updike the comparison is frequently relevant. Reviewing Hemingway's letters, for example, he calls on James and notes that Hemingway was the first novelist since James to think so much about "literary immortality and perfection of prose." Commenting on Edmund Wilson's journals, he wonders how Wilson's editor, Leon Edel, must feel about Wilson's bedroom antics after working so long with "the elegant leavings of Henry James." Writing about Saul Bellow's *The Dean's December*, he muses whether James might not have found Bellow's ethnic neighborhoods "a hopeless waste-land." Pointing to the hard sense of irrevocable change in Iris Murdoch's *Nuns and Soldiers*, he recalls "the immense, laconic exchange" at the conclusion of *The Wings of the Dove*. Describing Maurice Blanchot's style, he again calls on James's achievement to make the comparison: "Blanchot's prose gives an impression, like Henry James's, of carrying meanings so fragile they might crumble in transit."[8]

Throughout these remarks, made largely in the late 1970s and early 1980s, there is a sense that modern and contemporary novelists, no matter their innovations and accomplishments, are still aspiring while the nineteenth-century author has achieved. Reading Updike's nonfiction prose, I found only one significant comment

which suggests that James cannot measure up to a contemporary.
That writer, as expected, is Nabokov. As long ago as 1964, while
writing for *New Republic* (26 September 1964) and pointedly titling
his essay "Grandmaster Nabokov" as a means of echoing the name
given James, "the Master," Updike observed: "In the intensity of its
intelligence and reflective joy, his fiction is unique in this decade
and scarcely precedented in American literature. Melville and James
do not, oddly, offer themselves for comparison."[9] Two points may be
noted here. First, the opinion is a relatively early one and was apparently adjusted during the next two decades, not to the detriment
of Nabokov but to the appreciation of James. Second, in calling the
names of Melville and James, Updike indirectly suggests that of all
American novelists only these two are possible rivals for Nabokov's
eminence. He later reiterated his praise of James when, testifying
before the Subcommittee on Select Education of the House of Rep-
resentatives Committee on Education and Labor (30 January 1978),
he selected James along with Freud, Kafka, Proust, Joyce, and
Whitman as "brave, strange, stubborn spirits" who have "most brilliantly illuminated our sense of humanity." Still, Updike is aware—
and amused—that Nabokov glanced across from his own lofty van-
tage point to James's and dismissed the latter as "that pale porpoise
and his plush vulgarities."[10]

Although Updike smiles at Nabokov's witticism, he himself is not
always somber-faced when discussing James. "A Mild 'Complaint'"
is an example. Originally written in January 1961 but not published
until twenty-one years later (*New Yorker*, 19 April 1982), this short
spoof satirizes scholars who stumble all over themselves when in the
presence of the master's prose and thus inevitably clutter their commentaries with reverence in the guise of quotation marks around
nearly every other word. As Updike correctly notes, one cannot excuse these scholars with the argument that James's notorious late
style reveals its own punctuational excesses. James's effect is quite
different

> In James himself, these footless exclamation marks serve as a 'kind of
> spice' to the 'lavish feast' whose most 'delicious' ingredient is the
> host's visible relish in the 'fare' he is 'setting forth.' Whereas with the
> scholars 'barnacled' to the underside of his 'stately gliding' reputa-
> tion, the 'marks' are 'symptomatic of' a mere 'itch,' if for which an

appropriate cure, or at least 'implement for scratching,' can be located, I will, indeed, 'be grateful.'[11]

Updike, of course, makes fun of James too, but the parody is part of
the praise.

Several months later he developed his understanding of the relationship between parody and James. In an essay-review of Dwight
Macdonald's anthology *Parodies* (*New Yorker*, 16 September 1961),
he discusses the history of parody as a celebrated literary sidelight,
and he names James, Wordsworth, Browning, Whitman, and Hemingway as the five most-parodied authors in English. Not subject
matter but style is the focus of the fun. Like the other writers men-
tioned, James carries the peculiarities of his style to the edge of the
absurd. Thus the initiated reader can often detect the contrast between James's stylistic sophistication and his efforts to be colloquial.
Once again James's generous use of quotation marks is an issue:
"This is perhaps least plain in the case of James, but observe, in
Beerbohm's 'The Guerdon' and, scarcely diminuendo, in the late
James himself, how the scrupulously long sentences tiptoe forward
through the demisemiquavers of qualification to offer us, like a
dime-store locket on the end of the gold chain, some little cliché, or
trinket, mounted proudly in quotes, of contemporary 'idiom.'"[12] As
an example, I cite the following sentence, picked at random, from
The Golden Bowl. Adam Verver is the center of attention: "*This* was
the problem he had worked out to its solution—the solution that
was now doing more than all else to make his feet settle and his days
flush; and when he wished to feel 'good,' as they said at American
City, he had but to retrace his immense development."[13] Read in
isolation, the sentence with its quoted "good" is unremarkable, but
in the course of an eight-hundred-page novel the plethora of words
singled out is noticeable. James is not at his best when he tries to
echo the language of the street, but as Updike understands, no significant author is invulnerable to parody.

One of Updike's earliest published references to James is itself a
parody. In "Why Robert Frost Should Receive the Nobel Prize"
(*Audience*, Summer 1960), Updike, amid mock praise of Pearl Buck
and Somerset Maugham at the expense of authors he truly admires,
pokes fun at readers who long for the joys of simple literature and

who deprecate the achievements of such complex writers as Henry James, described here as "an agonized paralytic victim" of "the disease of endlessly pecking like nervous chickens at the wonderful and unified fabric of human experience."[14] The point is that Updike does not pontificate when celebrating James. A grin appears here; a laugh seems held in check there. In "The Author as Librarian" (*New Yorker*, 30 October 1965), he smiles at Borges's refreshing evaluation of James and H. G. Wells: "In connection with Wells and Henry James, it is a salutary shock to find the terms of the usual invidious comparison reversed: 'the sad and labyrinthine Henry James . . . a much more complex writer than Wells, although he was less gifted with those pleasant virtues that are usually called classical.'"[15]

In general, however, Updike admires the clarity of James's complexity. An unexpected bow in that direction occurs in, of all places, his review of a collection of Xingu Indian myths (*New Yorker*, 16 September 1974). Commenting on the "laconic closeness of event" in the primitive tales that renders them all but opaque, he again holds up the standard of James as a contrasting illustration of intricacy that offers several openings to the reader. Complexity joined with accessibility is a virtue: "One can skim a paragraph by Henry James, get the general picture, and either go back for the furniture and nuance or get on with the story. Skim a paragraph of these myths, and one is lost."[16] One may question if James rewards a skimmer, but one finds his difficulty accessible because James keeps his eyes on the real.

None of the above means that Updike's appreciation of James is uncritical. There are differences to be observed, variations to be considered. An early opinion from "Creatures of the Air" (*New Yorker*, 30 September 1961) illustrates his reservations. Evaluating Muriel Spark's novels, Updike notes the apparent ease with which such British authors as Trollope create solid novels out of a comment or a gesture. American authors, he suggests, do not fare so well when they try for similar results with similar material: "James' novels, for all their lovely furniture, remain pilgrim's progresses whose substance thins gaseously beyond the edges of the moral issue."[17] It is not that James chews more than he bites off but that, unlike Trollope, he is on surer ground when not the substantial furniture of the social scene but the abstract quality of the moral question shapes the center of his fiction. What Updike calls the "refinement of form" does not compensate for an insider's knowledge of how the gestures and glimpses—the furniture—add up.

James's status as an American observer of Anglicans may be a factor. While Updike glories in the ordinariness of the American middle class, James had to find his perspective in England. One result was that he was often the outsider looking in; looking in with delicacy and taste and perspicacity, of course, but nevertheless looking in. Thus in the following description of James's self-exile, Updike refers to James's notorious comments in *Hawthorne* and indirectly explains why he himself has stayed home:

> Henry James, writing of the young Hawthorne, imagined him gazing out upon a landscape of negatives: "No sovereign, no court . . . no country gentlemen, no palaces, no castles, no manors. . . ." By the time, in 1879, that James penned these words, rich Americans were aggressively supplying some of the lacks, including that of ivied ruins. . . . Perhaps the index of the degree of civilization which James found wanting in his native land lies less in the landscape's furniture than in the intensity of satisfaction with which the living population regard their surrounding of visible heritage.[18]

If Americans aggressively supply ruins, they artificially create heritage. James found intense but not aggressive satisfaction in the English cathedrals, the country houses, and the drawing rooms. Updike takes a similar satisfaction in the American surroundings of his visible heritage, but with the significant difference that his is composed of small churches and bedrooms. The mundane, what he calls the "grits, bumps, and anonymities" of middleness, are persistently present at the heart of his fiction.[19]

The anonymity of mundane particulars is for Updike an indication of spiritual reality. God, he argues, made trees and telephone poles equally well. James does not share Updike's sense of religious belief, but he would agree with Updike's insistence on the validation of reality by the observation of details. One of Updike's precise statements on this point is the conclusion of his early short story "The Blessed Man of Boston, My Grandmother's Thimble, and Fanning Island": "Just as a piece of turf torn from a meadow becomes a *gloria* when drawn by Dürer. Details. Details are the giant's fingers."[20] Details shape both what he calls the landscape's furniture and the characters who walk through the scene, and character shapes action.

The Jamesian virtue that Updike especially approves of is the realistic portrayal of character. Updike's commitment to realism is the linchpin of his art. As long ago as 1964, for instance, in a speech upon accepting the National Book Award for *The Centaur*, he remarked that he missed "in much contemporary writing, this sense of self-qualification, the kind of timid reverence toward what exists that Cézanne shows when he grapples for the shape and shade of a fruit through a mist of delicate stabs."[21] Nearly two decades later, in a speech when receiving the National Book Critics Circle Award for *Rabbit Is Rich* (delivered by his editor, Judith Jones, 28 January 1982), he expressed his appreciation for readers who respond to the ordinariness of what exists: "In an age when, as in most others, it is easier to cry crisis than to describe peace, I am touched that you have singled out for this recognition an unsensational rendering of equivocal normal life, as it is led in middle age, by a man as ordinary as any American is ordinary."[22]

These and other comments explain his approval of James's praise for Hawthorne's Zenobia that James first expressed in his book *Hawthorne*. In a speech on Hawthorne given before the American Academy and Institute of Arts and Letters (24 May 1979), Updike describes Zenobia as the "overwarm, perversely shunned heroine," and he cites James's statement that Zenobia is "the nearest approach that Hawthorne has made to the complete creation of a *person*. . . . I feel that his principle was wrong. . . . Imagination is out of place; only the strictest realism can be right."[23] Updike has in mind, of course, James's refusal to accept Hawthorne's distinction between Romance and realism, a refusal discussed in the previous chapter. Indeed, suggests Updike, James's early commitment to realism was so staunch that he felt uneasy whenever an author embellished the real. In "Whitman's Egotheism," a talk given at the Pierpont Morgan Library (4 October 1977), Updike recalls that the youthful James, reviewing Whitman's *Drum-Taps*, was unable to respond with a shock of recognition to the poet's celebration of the self. Noting that James called *Drum-Taps* "an offence against art," he wonders at the extremity of the censure: "The Whitmanesque pose is a thorough artifact, and, the duty of the artist being to make a virtue of necessity, Whitman is existentially artful at a depth far beyond the easy rhymers with whom James felt at home."[24] The issue for both Updike and James usually turns on the reality of a writer's fictional people. In a short but revealing observation Updike brings together three literary giants in one sentence to make his point: "Compared to Tolstoy's protagonists or those of Henry James, Joyce's characters do not take each other seriously."[25]

II

Although the creation of realistic characters in detailed domestic situations is a central factor for both Updike and James, the variations are as instructive as the similarities. In general neither author is more than passingly concerned with his characters' brush with historical forces. Some readers may name *The Princess Casamassima* and *Rabbit Redux* as novels in which large, impersonal concerns overwhelm sensitive participants, but the point is still that Updike and James narrow their fictional worlds in order to focus on small groups of people involved in often abstract matters that have the potential for huge consequences. James may chronicle the very rich while Updike details the suburban middle class, but war, poverty, race relations, political elections, and scientific advancements are not at issue; moral value, social intrigue, betrayal, innocence, and adultery are. Both novelists understand that the instability of their small domestic circles reflects a larger center that seems less than secure. Right and responsible action is nearly always the solution, but the dilemma is how to define the act.

For James—and I am speaking generally here—precise rendering of the "furniture" is normally in the service of evaluating the depths and ambiguities of character. The details surround significant issues that can be settled, not to the benefit of all concerned but at least to the extent that the social motion once again begins its whirl. Some problems are not solved and some characters are not satisfied, but what James would see as a necessary *social* harmony prevails at the end. Thus, while his characters are drawn with depth and resonance, his focus is also on the domestic intrigue that ensnares them. This is why the reader senses that the stability of the social contract, often a marriage, is more significant than the desires of the primary players. Isabel Archer may shrink from Gilbert Osmond, but fidelity to a social obligation is worth more than individual escape through adultery with Caspar Goodwood.

One closes a James novel with an understanding that while total happiness is denied, the characters hope to stride beyond a past of errors, heal the breach in the harmony, and step tentatively toward the future. James's adulterous characters do not sin so much as make mistakes that can be corrected. The complexity of the healing is illustrated in the following comment from the conclusion of *The Golden Bowl*: "The harmony was n't less sustained for being superficial" (2:358). Hypocrisy and deceit may be the cost exacted, but sustaining the superficial harmony is more critical than exposing the individual's wounds. James stresses the high-minded act because he insists on its possibility; the mundane is perhaps necessary but usually vulgar.

Since character flaw precipitates societal disruption, James isolates those who transgress the balance of moral value and social propriety; one thinks of Kate Croy, Charlotte Stant, and Mrs. Beale. Those who survive the domestic ordeal—often James's once-innocent heroines and "poor sensitive gentlemen"—touch the tragic because the alteration of their plans, schemes, or desires forces them to feel with Maggie Verver, usually for the first time, the "darkening shadow of a false position." Irony is thus James's primary tone. The potentially admirable characters do not always know what is going on. Once they find out, they adjust because they learn; what happens to the other characters is significant to them.

More often than not, the catalyst for the disrupting action is sexual in nature. Generally weak men become involved with generally strong women, and deceit rules the drawing room until order—no matter its superficiality—is renegotiated. Sir Claude (*What Maisie Knew*) and the Prince (*The Golden Bowl*) are physically desirable in the sense of sex equaling what Maggie calls the "sovereign power." James understands that submitting to that power signals a breach of contract when certain formalities are not observed. Violate the terms of an agreement and society totters just a bit more. Yet the sexual mandate is so persuasive that his characters often hurt each other. James's women are usually the antagonists because they are more determined within the enclosed domestic circles that serve as metaphors for society at large. Their determination gives them strength, which in turn gives them definition, and the best among them learn to keep their aspirations, sexual or otherwise, within the necessary, all-encompassing social harmony. Because James's characters accept in the end the limitations of their situations, they discover or return to their commitments. James seems confident about right and proper action. His endings are decisive if not final; and his superior people, superior by wealth or birth, assert their strength finally to restore the social balance. As Maggie says of Charlotte and the Prince, "They thought of everything but that I might think" (2:332).

Except for Rabbit Angstrom, Updike's sensitive characters spend too much time analyzing their own predicaments. They become so embroiled in the confusions of the individual self that they have trouble adjusting to the social consequences of their acts. Spiritual as well as social disaster hovers at the periphery of their obligations. Like James's minute notations, Updike's details of familial conflict are carefully observed and precisely rendered, but Updike does not share James's certainty that the dissension can be resolved, if only superficially. His moral dilemmas normally highlight not the public scene but one character, and thus the domestic intrigue that ensnares the character is more the setting than the issue. This is why the reader suspects that the demands of the social contract—spouse, children, job—are little more than restraining rules in a kind of suburban game that one may manipulate. Jerry Conant (*Marry Me*) feels obligated to his wife and kids, but fidelity to his personal sense of spiritual worth is more insistent, even if adultery is the only release for the pressure.

One puts down an Updike novel with the understanding that happiness generally is not possible. His characters are always dissatisfied because the grace that they once felt is lost somewhere in the past while the assurance that they seek is beckoning forever from the future. The complexity of the dilemma is illustrated in the following comment from *Marry Me*: "Maybe our trouble is that we live in the twilight of the old morality, and there's just enough to torment us, and not enough to hold us in."[26] Guilt is the natural result of such a quandary, but unlike James, Updike does not believe that the breach in the harmony can be healed. His characters publicly ex-

pose their wounds with a masochistic relish. Rather than concede to
an act that would be defined as high-minded within the terms of
social propriety, they settle for an individual response. James would
appreciate Rabbit's predicament as defined at the conclusion of *Rabbit, Run*, but he would not applaud Rabbit's solution: "On this small
fulcrum he tries to balance the rest, weighing opposites against each
other: Janice and Ruth, Eccles and his mother, the right way and
the good way."[27] Rabbit chooses the good over the right, and the
imperative "run" in the title hints that his creator supports his
choice.

Like James, Updike understands that such flawed characters dis-
rupt the harmony, but he does not punish those who upset the balance. Updike offers little true chastisement because he views his
transgressors more as aspirers toward an undefined goal of freedom
and fluidity (what Rabbit calls "it") than as serious violators of the
social contract. One thinks of Tom Marshfield (*A Month of Sundays*) and Jerry Conant. So long as they believe, in theologian Karl
Barth's sense of the word, that man cannot reach God but only God
can touch man, they may be hurt but not punished. Those who
come through the domestic ordeal—usually modernized versions of
James's poor sensitive gentlemen—rarely graze the tragic because
they see their crises more in individual than in societal terms. Nostalgia is thus often Updike's pervasive tone. Aspiring rather than accepting, his adulterers glance over their shoulders at an Edenlike
perfection that they think they once had and forward to a transcendence that they hope they may gain. Unlike James's protagonists,
Updike's do not change much because they are usually in the process of learning. What happens to the other characters is relatively
unimportant to them except as they themselves are affected.

Updike agrees with James that sex normally precipitates the action. His unsettled men marry physically uninspiring women who
seem to thrust them toward eternal blankness. Rabbit, Piet Hanema
(*Couples*), and Joey Robinson (*Of the Farm*) think constantly about
sex, but unlike James's understanding of the "sovereign power"
there is little sense of supremacy about them. They pursue sex to
hold off stasis and death. Updike also shares James's conviction that
adultery is a violation of contract, but he considers the transgression
more an individual than an ethical or legal matter. Break a contract

in Updike's marriage novels and society may shift, but personal salvation is more in jeopardy despite sincere efforts to avoid causing pain. Those who do get hurt are Updike's women. Like James's, his are strong, but they are also stolid where Kate Croy and Charlotte Stant are exciting. Updike's females merely react to their husbands' wanderings. Except for the persistent mother in *Of the Farm* (who is no longer sexual) and the determined wife in *Marry Me* (who is Updike's finest female character), his women are strong primarily because their men—dreamers all—are weak. This imbalance may illustrate the lack of cohesiveness that Updike finds in contemporary society; the enduring women are satellites to the usually weak but always aspiring men.

Contrary to James's characters, who finally accept personal limitations for the good of the social contract, Updike's turn to daydreams and the imagination. Because Updike is not as confident about right and proper action, he leaves his characters still trying to renegotiate their obligations. The endings of his marriage novels are therefore not decisive because, despite persistent battering, the dreams are still intact at the conclusion. His good yet flawed people have not wealth or bloodline to sustain them but sensitivity and a measure of insight which they usually cannot express. Maggie Verver is correct when she says that her antagonists thought of everything except that she might think, but Rabbit and Piet and Jerry have to rely on feeling as well as reflection. They do not have the Jamesian capacity for thought.

III

Pursuit of the other sex involves the characters of Updike and James in the complications of what may be called contractual obligations. Despite the difference between their characters' bank accounts, the question both authors raise is not merely who loves whom but also how the answer to that query affects the economic, spiritual, and familial agreements of the lovers. A general truth that fiction has apparently taken from history is that contracts and violation of them are inextricable. All social boundaries, whether sanctioned by legal documents or blessed by religious vows, are made to be crossed. An obsession to violate the boundary is what Tony

Tanner identifies as the secret interest of the bourgeois novel: "It has indeed followed the fortunes, and changes, of the family, and as we all too well know, one of its abiding topics has been the progress toward marriage. Yet it is my contention that its real, if secret, interest has been aroused by the weak points in the family, the possible fissures, the breaches, the breakdowns. Which is why the novel tends to be drawn, all but irresistibly, to the problem of adultery."[28]

The point is that the unstable trio of adultery rather than the static duet of marriage is the generative form not only in the novel but also in Western literature. Yet adultery has what Tanner calls "special importance" in the late eighteenth- and nineteenth-century novel because in detailing the institution of marriage novelists finally expose its instability. Adultery threatens the social order by admitting multiplicity (mistress, lover) to the unity of socially defined roles (wife, husband), so much so that the word *adulteress* carries connotations of adulteration and pollution (12). The adulteress, or, even worse, the unfaithful wife and thus bad mother, is nearly always more severely castigated in fiction than the wayward man. Since society bands together to ostracize threats to its well-being, which depends on order and stability, however superficial, it will attempt to make the adulteress a nonperson by equating her with the negative of everything good. Hester Prynne, created by the author who stands in the background of both James and Updike, is the classic example of the socially spurned woman in American literature.

When Maggie manipulates her family to force Charlotte Stant back to America, she is banishing her sexually active former friend *and* stepmother to a state of negativity. Despite Charlotte's access to a fortune through the good offices of her husband, Maggie's father, her exile to the United States carries with it echoes of Hester's banishment to the cabin in the clearing near the forest. Since Charlotte detests America, she can suffer no more damning punishment. It is crucial that Maggie does not expose Charlotte's adultery and thus require her to wear Hester's A, but the fact remains that in the United States she will be a nonentity so far as the Prince is concerned. Only Europeans appreciate the quality that allows Charlotte definition—her high style. Americans, James implies, care primarily for morality and little for manners. They view contracts as obligations to be met.

The specter of adultery is more potent in the fiction of James's age than are revealing accounts of the disordering act itself. This generalization defines a specific contrast between James and Updike even though they examine similar material. Once the adulterous act is literally described in fiction, as it is more and more in the twentieth century, society's outcry loses effectiveness. For Tanner the results of this change of direction in the novel are more dire than perhaps is the case: "The bourgeois novel of adultery finally discovers its own impossibility, and as a result sexuality, narration, and society fall apart, never to be reintegrated in the same way—if, indeed, at all" (14). Tanner calls these kinds of novels "post-social fictional forms," and thus in his one reference to Updike he argues that while *Couples* describes adulteries, it is not a novel of adultery:

> When a society ceases to care much about marriage, and all that is implied in that transaction, by the same token it will lose contact with the sense of intense passion. This would mean that the novel of adultery, as I have been describing it, would vanish—as indeed it has. A novel like John Updike's *Couples* is as little about passion as it is about marriage; the adulteries are merely formal and technical. Adultery, we may say, no longer signifies. (89)

Not everyone agrees, of course. One remembers that even on the popular front *Time* magazine (26 April 1968) greeted *Couples* with a cover story on Updike and a banner that proclaimed "the adulterous society." And Updike himself has insisted on the connection between adultery and fiction. Norman Cousins paraphrases Updike's response to a startled group of Soviet authors: "He quoted the French as saying that the novel cannot exist without adultery. Readers, he said, tend to be quickly sated with tales involving fame or wealth."[29] More pointedly, Updike defines the bourgeois novel as erotic. In "If at First You Do Succeed, Try, Try Again" (*New Yorker*, 10 April 1971), he describes the kind of novel that he and James write and that Tanner apparently calls for. Note his emphasis on contract: "The bourgeois novel is inherently erotic, just as the basic unit of bourgeois order—the family unit built upon the marriage contract—is erotic. Who loves whom? Once this question seems less than urgent, new kinds of novels must be written, or none at all."[30] Tanner's opinion of Updike's marriage novels must be evaluated within his definition of the novel of adultery, but it also suggests a conservative description of the genre of fiction and of the subject matter that one accepts as suitable for it. For Tanner the novels of Updike (or for that matter Lawrence, Joyce, etc.) illustrate that society, sexuality, and narration have lost their cohesiveness, but one could also argue that modern fiction is not a harbinger of destruction for the art form but a sign of how the genre rejuvenates itself through adaptation and change. Beginning where traditional novels of manners used to end—with marriage—fiction like *Couples* must consider primarily the threats to the signed contract.

The key difference between *Couples* and *The Golden Bowl* is not that Updike describes the bedroom while James tiptoes past the door but that Updike's characters judge marriage primarily as a spiritual vow while James's see it as a social contract. Both novelists balance law and sympathy, which is generally the case in traditional novels, but for Updike the law has little to do with agreements in the legal sense. His transgressors, often male, worry for their souls; James's, often female, worry for their propriety. Tanner correctly observes that marriage is "*the* central subject" for the novel because society defines marriage as "the all-subsuming, all-organizing, all-containing contract" (15). The contract encompasses everything: family loyalty, personal libido, private property, and children. To threaten the marital contract, as Charlotte Stant does, is to challenge the foundations of society. Banishment of the one is necessary to preserve the harmony of the other. To threaten the religious contract, as Jerry Conant does, is to challenge the spiritual salvation of the soul. Banishment is also necessary—Jerry to his imagination, Piet to another suburb,` Marshfield to the omega-shaped motel in the desert—but society itself is hardly in jeopardy.

Thus what I understand to be Updike's contribution to the novel of marriage and adultery is what Tanner judges a breakdown: "We may say that as the contract between man and wife loses its sense of necessity and binding power, so does the contract between novelist and reader" (15). The James of the major phase may be the turning point. By the time of *The Golden Bowl* the legal contract between the Prince and Maggie requires accommodation by both parties. He must adjust his heritage of being a "grand man" to her understanding of moral commitment, and she must adapt the watertight compartments of her morality to his understanding of high style. Neither mentions his adultery with Charlotte. To do so would be publicly to expose the breach. Yet for both James and Updike marriage and its necessity, not seduction and its delights, are the main subjects. Piet and Joey do remarry, and Tom Marshfield presumably returns to his wife. Only Jerry Conant continues to waffle at the end; as he observes about the connection between his wife and his soul: "I'm married to my death." That the contract is more a spiritual vow than a legal document in Updike's fiction is not a sign that the novel has broken down but a variation that the novel has absorbed. Who loves whom is as much the issue in Updike as it is in James, Howells, Hawthorne, and even Charles Brockden Brown. The threat of adultery is crucial to them all.

The paradox is that while absence of adultery may threaten the novel, adultery itself threatens society. Perhaps the most spectacular destruction wrought by illicit passion is in the *Iliad*. Tanner is direct: "Western literature as we know it starts with an act of transgression" (24). Not only are families split apart and countries hurled into war as a result of Paris's seduction of Helen, but the universe itself is jeopardized when even the gods join the fray. Calamity of this magnitude is possible in the epic. James and Updike cannot consider such extremes of disaster, but they understand that society rests on order and that order is preserved by law. The far side of adultery may be chaos, but where the chaos is universal for Homer and social for James, it is individual for Updike. In each case, however, a similar question is posed: If marriage is the epitome of social form, what happens when the form begins to shatter? Is it possible, in other words, to have Maggie's golden bowl without the crack?

The answer, James implies, may be acceptance of both the crack and the gilt that covers it from public scrutiny. The Prince, for example, knows that his financial well-being depends on Maggie's commitment to the superficial harmony. Much more than Updike's philanderers he recognizes the bonds between the rules of marriage and the realities of economic stability. He may care for Maggie, but he has, after all, married her for the security that her thumping bank account guarantees. If money were not an issue with him, he would have married Charlotte. In this sense James is very much aware of society's dependence on the wedding vow. Fractured mar-

5. "Why Write?" 34.

6. John Updike, "Notes of a Temporary Resident," *Picked-Up Pieces* 44.

7. John Updike, "One Big Interview," *Picked-Up Pieces* 500.

8. *Hugging the Shore* 171–72, 207, 262, 356, 544.

9. John Updike, "Grandmaster Nabokov," *Assorted Prose* (New York: Knopf, 1965) 319.

10. *Hugging the Shore* 869, 220.

11. *Hugging the Shore* 69.

12. John Updike, "Beerbohm and Others," *Assorted Prose* 252.

13. Henry James, *The Golden Bowl*, 2 vols. (New York: Scribner's, 1909) 1:149. Hereafter cited parenthetically.

14. *Assorted Prose* 29.

15. *Picked-Up Pieces* 174.

16. *Picked-Up Pieces* 477.

17. *Assorted Prose* 307.

18. John Updike, "New England Churches" (written as a foreword to Robert Mutrux, *Great New England Churches* [Chester, CT: Globe Pequot Press, 1982]), *Hugging the Shore* 64–65.

19. John Updike, foreword, *Olinger Stories* (New York: Vintage, 1964) vii.

20. John Updike, "The Blessed Man of Boston, My Grandmother's Thimble, and Fanning Island," *Pigeon Feathers* (New York: Knopf, 1962) 245.

21. John Updike, "Accuracy," *Picked-Up Pieces* 17.

22. *Hugging the Shore* 876.

23. John Updike, "Hawthorne's Creed," *Hugging the Shore* 77, 79.

24. *Hugging the Shore* 110.

25. John Updike, "Questions Concerning Giacomo," *Picked-Up Pieces* 161.

26. John Updike, *Marry Me: A Romance* (New York: Knopf, 1976) 53.

27. John Updike, *The Poorhouse Fair/Rabbit, Run* (New York: Modern Library, 1965) 433. This is the first revised American edition.

28. Tony Tanner, *Adultery in the Novel: Contract and Transgression* (Baltimore: Johns Hopkins University Press, 1979) 371. Hereafter cited parenthetically.

29. Norman Cousins, "When American and Soviet Writers Meet," *Saturday Review* 24 June 1978:42.

30. *Picked-Up Pieces* 402.

2　Updike and Hawthorne

pdike's response to the achievement of Henry James is more complex but less formal than his opinion of Hawthorne. Although he celebrates Hawthorne's fiction, he does not hold up the author of *The Scarlet Letter* as the standard for later American novelists to emulate. More important, his remarks about Hawthorne lack the focus on such matters as domestic detail and portrayal of character. These differences do not mean, however, that Hawthorne is a negligible predecessor for Updike. In several scattered observations he nods in Hawthorne's direction, and in a major essay he articulates his understanding of Hawthorne's art. While that essay is not as extensive as James's 1879 book on Hawthorne, it is nevertheless a significant statement about the primary area where Updike and Hawthorne meet: the inextricable unity of religion, sexual transgression, and guilt. Erotic desire and religious sensibility shape the centers of their fiction. A look at Updike's secondary references to·Hawthorne will set the frame for an examination of his important essay on the author of *The Scarlet Letter* and *The Marble Faun*.

Curiously, few references to Hawthorne appear in Updike's nonfiction prose before the 1970s. One of the first allusions, for example, is found in a foreword to a reprint of Oscar Wilde's *The Young King and Other Tales* (New York: Macmillan, 1962). Updike merely names Hawthorne as an author who created stories for children with as much seriousness and wisdom as he wrote for adults. The most significant early mention is in his review of Muriel Spark's *The Bachelors* (*New Yorker*, 30 September 1961), where he cites Hawthorne before initiating a comparison of Spark and James: "Since Hawthorne praised Trollope's novels as 'solid, substantial . . . as real as if some giant had hewn a great lump out of the earth and put it under a glass case,' American writers have coveted the assurance that enables their British counterparts to build persuasively and at length upon the overheard, the glimpsed, and the guessed."[1] Nearly two decades later, in an essay titled "Hawthorne's Creed," Updike developed his understanding of how Hawthorne relied on fantasy and symbol to suggest the impingement of the impalpable on the real, but in 1961 he did little more than cite Hawthorne's lament at being unable to fashion Trollope's solid lumps, and point out James's similar difficulty when straying beyond the edges of the moral issue toward the substantial furniture of the domestic scene.

Updike's later commentary gives thanks that Hawthorne avoided the lumps. In 1972 he coined a delightful phrase to describe Hawthorne as a "fusty old wizard" ("Satires without Serifs," *New Yorker*, 13 May 1972), and in a 1965 essay on Borges ("The Author as Librarian," *New Yorker*, 30 October 1965), he commented on the Argentine author's attraction to the "oneiric and hallucinatory quality" in certain North American writers, especially Hawthorne and Whitman.[2] One notes the contrast with James, who, in his own remarks on Hawthorne, questioned the earlier author's embellishment of reality. Updike clearly agrees with Borges, and he underscores what twentieth-century readers have come to celebrate—Hawthorne's need to graft fantasy onto the mundane roots of the real. Remarking that, along with Melville, Hawthorne was one of Nabokov's two favorite American novelists, he regrets that Nabokov never lectured on them.[3]

When Updike does urge Hawthorne as a standard of excellence for struggling novelists to look toward, he refers to African writers and to his own imaginary character Henry Bech. In "Out of the Glum Continent" (*New Yorker*, 13 November 1971), an essay detailing the efforts of contemporary African authors to deal with the complexities of their dark heritage, he suggests an analogy to the first great writers in the United States, calls *The Scarlet Letter* "our own first masterpiece," and describes it as "scarcely a paean to the past." Similarly, he recommends Hawthorne to Henry Bech. Commenting on Bech's tormented drive for literary recognition, he muses on the eternity of "that high, calm pool of immortality where Proust and Hawthorne and Catullus float, glassy-eyed and belly-up."[4] They may be dead, but they have earned what Bech covets.

I

These comments would not be worth remembering were it not for the extensive attention Updike gave to Hawthorne in the late 1970s and early 1980s. One wonders if, unlike his consistent appreciation of James, he had to cultivate his affinity with Hawthorne. If so, the cultivation was worth the wait, for it encourages a serious consideration of the relationship between the contemporary dissector of suburbia and the New England authority on guilt. Writing his essay on Melville, for example, Updike had to recall Hawthorne. In these remarks, originally delivered as a lecture on 23 October 1981 before being revised for publication (*New Yorker*, 10 May 1982), he uses such words as "stimulated" and "emboldened" to describe Hawthorne's impact on the author of *Moby-Dick*; and while it is clear that Updike is not as enraptured of his forerunner as was Melville, it is nevertheless significant that Hawthorne is now one of his primary points of reference. He is aware, for instance, that unlike Hawthorne (and himself), Melville "did not receive what might have been psychologically useful at this time—a fully generous public salute from a high-minded peer, such as he had given Hawthorne."[5] Yet Updike also understands that unlike Melville (and himself), Hawthorne labored in obscurity before the glow of public recognition revealed the secret of his greatness. Updike pictures the undiscovered Hawthorne as "the young hermit of Salem" using journals to step into "the light of print," and he refers, of course, to Hawthorne's early tales which he describes as "seductive and limpid."[6]

One year after the Melville essay Updike reviewed John Cheever's last novel and clarified his sense of Hawthorne's seductiveness. In "On Such a Beautiful Green Little Planet" (*New Yorker*, 5 April 1982), he notes how in such authors as Cheever and Hawthorne the instinctive acceptance of creation accompanies "an inevitable sensitivity to corruption." In an eye-catching phrase typical of his best critical remarks, Updike caps his comparison of the two writers by calling them "poet[s] of the poisoned."[7] Reading that description with its pointed reminder of the proximity of art and pain, one thinks of "Rappaccini's Daughter" and its eerie marriage of poisoned science, sexual nuance, and religious imagery. The union of guilt, sex, and belief is what finally attracts Updike to Hawthorne, and his most penetrating discussion of the relationship appears in "Hawthorne's Creed," the essay in which he discusses Hawthorne's moral reaction to the kind of transgression that James responded to from a social perspective.

Updike tinkered with the essay for several years. Originally titled "Hawthorne's Religious Language" and delivered as a lecture to the American Academy and Institute of Arts and Letters on 24 May 1979, the talk was then published in the *Proceedings* of the Academy and Institute (Second Series, Number 30). Updike later revised his comments and published them as an essay, "On Hawthorne's Mind," in the *New York Review of Books* (19 March 1981). Subsequently in 1981, Targ Editions printed the essay as "Hawthorne's Creed" in a collector's edition of 250 numbered copies, signed. The essay was then slightly revised again and included in *Hugging the Shore* (1983).

Updike looks to Hawthorne and asks the question that his own sensitive gentlemen pose to themselves: What did Hawthorne believe? That the author of *The Scarlet Letter*, "our classic novel of religious conscience and religious suffering," boasted of not attending church is a curiosity worth investigating. Updike quotes Julian Hawthorne on the matter: Hawthorne's faith was "somehow apparent," but he "never discussed religion in set terms either in his writing or in his talk." Perhaps the closest he came to outright expression of his religious beliefs is the essay "Sunday at Home," in which he assures the reader (and himself?) that while doubt and evil may beckon close, he takes heart that his soul has never "lost the instinct of its faith. . . . Though my form be absent, my inner man goes constantly to church."[8]

As Updike points out, Hawthorne's religious waffling was not unusual in the first half of the nineteenth century. With Protestantism spawning a bewildering variety of doctrines from the Shakers to the Swedenborgians, an intellectual such as Hawthorne might have easily declined the outward trappings of ceremony while accepting the piety of the age. Neither pagan like Whitman nor prophet like Emerson, he used his fiction to examine his doubts. Questions of belief intensified as his career progressed. Updike calls this development Hawthorne's "involuntary creed": "a very vivid ghost of Christianity stares out at us from his prose, alarming and odd in not being evenly dead, but alive in some limbs and amputate in others, blurred in some aspects and otherwise basilisk-keen."[9]

With this said, however, the original question remains: What did Hawthorne believe? The query intrigues Updike because he as well as his male characters consider the answers to similar questions vital to their lives. Rabbit Angstrom, for example, believes in "it," the good way (freedom) as opposed to the right way (wife), and Updike himself accepts the strictures of Karl Barth's unblinking insistence on the first tenet of the Apostles' Creed ("I believe in God the Father"). But Hawthorne, suggests Updike, might define his own creed by describing himself as "delicate, fragile, and threatened," and by identifying "the menace of the world with the Puritanism of his ancestors." Updike reads much of Hawthorne's canon as a progressive weaning from the Puritan chain of command. From Hester's dismissal of "these iron men, and their opinions," through the defeat of Dimmesdale and the death of Judge Pyncheon, to Hollingsworth in *The Blithedale Romance* is a long way. Updike sympathizes with the well-known statement in "The Artist of the Beautiful": the "hard, brute force darkens and confuses the spiritual element within me."[10] Puritanism personified in these iron gray men is the hard brute force.

To appreciate what the gradual melting of the iron means to Updike's fiction, one should consider the Reverend Tom Marshfield's gradual seduction of his future wife in *A Month of Sundays*. Updike's tone in this novel is comic, but the general crisis, a minister's lapse of faith in the face of humanism and erotic desire, is quite serious. Unlike Dimmesdale and Hawthorne, Marshfield has Karl Barth's rigorous theology to sustain him. Aware, with Barth, that staunch acceptance of ethical principles will not alleviate human problems, Marshfield can criticize his liberal and socially involved wife: "She was moderate, I extreme. She was liberal and ethical and soft, I Barthian and rather hard."[11] If ethical behavior is not good enough, how far may a sexually aroused but true believer roam? Dimmesdale must pose a similar question when he finds himself in the forest with Hester Prynne. Marshfield acts when he decides that the an-

swer to his query is "pretty far," and Dimmesdale dallies when he
does not meet Hester again for seven years, but both plunge toward
the abyss.

Marshfield initially confronts the Hawthornian dichotomy of sex
and belief when, as a theology student, he courts the daughter of
Professor of Ethics Wesley Augustus Chillingworth. The name is a
deliberate howler, of course, but the combined allusions to St.
Augustine's lust before conversion, John Wesley's Methodism, and
Roger Chillingworth's impotence indicate the confusion Updike attributes to those who elevate ethics over belief. The progression
that he identifies in Hawthorne's serious effort to divorce himself
from the grip of implacable Puritanism is reflected comically in
Marshfield's determination to seduce Jane Chillingworth while
groping with her in a room directly above the study of the Professor
of Ethics. Marshfield's progress toward orgasm follows Chillingworth's syllabus for the course:

> By spring we had won through to Grotius and his *jus gentium*, and as
> modern ethics unfolded under Chillingworth's muttering I had the
> parallel pleasure, as it were in running footnote, of seducing his
> daughter. We met in the cool British sunshine of Hobbesian realism
> . . . and agreed to play again, as partners. By the time of our next
> date, Hume was exploding "ought" and "right" and Bentham was at-
> tempting to reconstruct hedonism with maximization formulas. Our
> first kiss came during Spinoza, more *titillatio* than *hilaritus*. . . . As
> Kant attempted to soften rationalism with categorical imperatives
> and *Achtung*, Jane let me caress her breast through her sweater. By
> the time of Hegel's monstrous identification of morality with the de-
> mands of the state, my hand was hot in her bra, and my access had
> been universalized to include her thighs.[12]

The tour de force continues for several more pages. Hawthorne
might be less explicit, but his gradual attempt to extricate himself
from Puritanism was as steady as Marshfield's progressive dismissal
of ethics. Surely Updike has Dimmesdale in mind, however ironically, in the description of the climax of the scene. Note the final
sentence: "Chillingworth would dustily cough beneath us at the
oddest moments, so often in synchrony with orgasm as to suggest
telepathic discomfort. I was slaying him that the Lord might live."
Ethical humanism cannot stand before the mandate of belief, and

Marshfield is a true Barthian believer. Rabbit will run and Marshfield will philander, but both keep the faith despite distracting ministrations from Reverend Eccles and Professor Chillingworth. Significantly, a silent but sexually adept nurse named Ms. Prynne teaches Marshfield how to reconcile body and soul.

Updike's other male characters long for a similar reconciliation. Hoping to find it in the bed of a desirable woman, they know that adultery may nurture guilt, but it also holds off threats to the annihilation of the spirit. Still, one might question Updike's inclination to justify adultery with the protection of belief as an effort to appease the body while reassuring the soul—as a wish, in short, to have his theistic cake and eat it. Adultery thus spices the staleness of monogamy, confronts the entropy of the marital contract, and does not bar the believer-as-transgressor from the church house door. Such a reservation would be worrisome if Updike joined Hawthorne in insisting on the separation of the corrupt body from the pristine soul, but his fiction shows just the opposite. Rather than maintain the gap, his characters long to close it as a means of reaffirming the unity that their Puritan forefathers rent. Hawthorne may be more rigorous and systematic in his probing of the dilemma, but Updike's lighter touch and uneasy defense of adultery do not mean that the problem of sex and belief is less serious for him than it is for Hawthorne. His adulterers are not as ready as Hawthorne's to discover the negative in the material. For Hawthorne, writes Updike, "matter verges upon being evil; virtue, upon being insubstantial." Pretty but less-than-erotic heroines are the result. As readers from the 1840s to today have noted, many of Hawthorne's acceptable women are as unbelievable in their purity as they seem insubstantial in their bodies. Faced with this dualism in Hawthorne, this split between body and soul, Updike argues that his predecessor's "insistence on delicate, ethereal heroines goes against not only our modern grain but his own as well—for in *The Blithedale Romance* it seems clear that it is not the ectoplasmic Priscilla the narrator loves, as the last sentence proclaims in capitals, but the dark, sensual, and doomed Zenobia. . . . The novel in its smallest details conveys Hawthorne's instinctive tenet that matter and spirit are inevitably at war."[13] One might add for illustration the community's demand that Hester hide her luxurious hair or the telling difference between the ethereal Hilda and the erotic Miriam in *The Marble Faun*.

Updike often characterizes his women to posit similar contrasts between the insubstantial but safe wife and the predatory but erotic mistress—witness the suggestive names of Piet Hanema's women in *Couples*, Angela (wife) and Foxy (mistress). For a moment Piet might be back in the pages of *The Marble Faun*, committed to Hilda in her protective tower while longing for Miriam in her dark catacombs. But the significant difference is that Updike's male characters finally shrink from fidelity to the delicate female because marriage brings stasis and stasis promises death. If Hawthorne's moral narrator of *The Blithedale Romance* "sometimes" closes his eyes when confronted with Zenobia's "full bust—in a word, her womanliness incarnated" because "it were not quite the privilege of modesty to gaze at her," Updike's Piet will choose Foxy over Angela even to the extreme of sucking the former's milk-filled breasts. Recall Jerry Conant's cry to his wife, the long-suffering Ruth, in *Marry Me*: "I'm married to my death."

For Updike adultery is often a social embarrassment but rarely a cause for individual damnation. Salvation is usually a personal matter of belief. The tension between loyalty to the wife and longing for the mistress fosters a guilt that in turn promises not the fires of hell but the pain of anguish. Domestic laceration is genuinely suffered in his fiction to the extent that the transgressor fears for his faith, and it is in this understanding of the relationship between erotic power and religious sensibility that Updike and Hawthorne join forces.

A primary difference is the punishment exacted. Hurl the charge of sexual transgressor against Rabbit, Piet, Jerry, or Marshfield, and they will retreat to the next suburb or even to their imaginations. Guilt maps their exile, and pain shapes their realization that they have exposed grievous domestic suffering, but they worry far more for themselves than for the stability of society or the morality of the family hearth. No one in Updike's fiction is damned to wear the A. In Hawthorne, however, the A seems eternal. Hester's letter adorns first her breast and last her tomb. It little matters that the A signals everything from adulteress to angel; Hawthorne's point is that Hester's iron men cannot forgive her as Christ forgave the woman taken in adultery. As for Dimmesdale, the ambiguous mark on his chest is as indelible as Hester's. The same stain defines them both. Unable to reconcile erotic desire and religious demands, Dimmesdale returns from his two trips to the forest first an adulterer and then a potential defiler of adolescent girls. Hawthorne will have him suffer no matter which way he turns. When he joins Hester in the forest, he violates a social and a spiritual commandment; when he ignores Hester in the town, he violates a personal need. The same is true in *The Marble Faun*, where Hawthorne offers either Hilda tending the Virgin's flame or Miriam fleeing the model's gaze. Body and soul, sex and salvation, are perpetually at odds. To give in to the former is to brand oneself with the eternal stain of blasphemy. To accept the latter is to damn oneself to an eternal state of frustration.

Updike argues that such absence of harmony is at the heart of both Hawthorne's creed and his fiction: "Where the two incompatible realms of Hawthorne's universe impinge, something leaks through; there is a *stain*. A sensation of blasphemous overlapping, of some vast substance chemically betraying itself, is central to the Gothic tradition of which Hawthorne's tales are lovely late blooms."[14] The stain, what Updike calls "this sinister spillage from another world," takes its form in the A on Hester's breast, the mark on Dimmesdale's chest, the blood in Colonel Pyncheon's throat, and any amount of dreams, potions, and mirrors. Updike has a point when he suggests that the insistent symbolism in Hawthorne, from the forests of the early tales through the sculpture and paintings in *The Marble Faun*, illustrates Hawthorne's understanding of a "potential invasion of the inanimate by the animate. . . . An aura of supernatural puppetry, of imminent spontaneous generation, haunts his tales."[15] Updike avoids such urgent symbols, but one cannot help noting that he learned Hawthorne's lesson well when he indicates the disturbing overlapping of body and soul in the form of the cock atop the phallic steeple of the Congregational church in *Couples*. Young people glance at the cock and see God. Hawthorne's characters cannot erase the stain; to remove it, as in "The Birthmark," is to die. But in *Couples* Updike's adulterers watch the church burn, find the cock rescued, and then move to the neighboring town. What Hawthorne might consider a fire of apocalypse, Updike shows to be merely a sign that his transgressor has fallen from the Edenic greenhouse of his parents to the hard rock of the world. From Angela to Foxy, angel to animal, is as close as the next bedroom.

Updike insists, then, and especially in *A Month of Sundays*, that body and soul, sex and religion, can unite. The tension in his fiction is often based on efforts to achieve the unity, whereas the dilemma in Hawthorne's is often determined by efforts to maintain the separation. Who loves whom is an issue for both, but Updike points to a line from Hawthorne's *English Notebooks*: "I cannot consent to let Heaven and Earth, this world and the next, be beaten up together like the white and yolk of an egg." Thus Updike finds two "sacred" ideas from Calvinism haunting Hawthorne's mind, providence and guilt: "Providence seems to be his sensation of inner delicacy projected outward upon the universe, where it is threatened by human monomania."[16] Populating his fiction with single-minded scientists, doctors, and experimenters, Hawthorne maintains that obsession disrupts the universe. Individuals and social circles are equally upset by monomania, just as James and Updike also show them to be, but for different reasons.

Of the second idea sacred to Calvinism—guilt—Updike notes that while Hawthorne was a connoisseur of guilt, he let it pervade "his work without any corroborating conviction of sin." In the reader's eyes Hester, Dimmesdale, and Miriam do not seem to be guilty of anything more than, as Hawthorne writes, striking out against "the moral gloom of the world." Their punishments are out of line with their transgressions. Yet a crucial point is that if the reader does not sense the seriousness of the characters' violations, they themselves most certainly do. They scrub at their stains, notes Updike, "under a Providence too delicately balanced to offer absolution." Convinced of their ineradicable sins, most of them die or wither or leave. Of Hawthorne's major wayward characters, only the antiseptic Hilda absolves the stain of witnessing a murder. But Updike, the reader, and presumably Hawthorne know that her absolution is unconvincing because she is a Puritan accepting the solace of a Roman Catholic confessional. Her greater sin looms as lurid as ever—denying Miriam sympathy—but Hawthorne does not seem to be concerned about that failing. Updike's summation of Hawthorne is perceptive: "He believed, with his Puritan ancestors, that man's spirit matters; that the soul can be distorted, stained, and lost; that the impalpable exerts force against the material."[17] Updike would perhaps agree with Hawthorne but with the crucial difference that while adultery may be a transgression, it does not doom the violator to the twin states of eternal separation of body and spirit and of earthly separation from human sympathy.

II

Only in the forest, beyond the sanctions of society, can the separation be overcome, but to venture there invites great peril. Adultery beckons but society judges. *The Scarlet Letter* details what Updike and James later reject: that the social order has not only the legal but also the moral authority to punish the woman taken in adultery. Since the Puritans equate law and religion, they must shrink from the threat to their social and moral structure that adultery promises. Yet with characteristic ambiguity Hawthorne shades the meanings so that one wonders if Hester's adultery is not an act of affirmation in an atmosphere of sterility. She creates while her accusers negate, and the result is that the first great adulteress in American literature is also the first great artist figure.

Hester's public sin of erotic freedom and her secret sin of intellectual curiosity ("She assumed a freedom of speculation, then common enough on the other side of the Atlantic, but which our forefathers, had they known of it, would have held to be a deadlier crime than that stigmatized by the scarlet letter"[18]) pale before her personal sin of silently permitting her husband to destroy her lover until he is too frail to be saved by her warning. Her guilt is not the result of sex but the product of secrecy. And her greatest secret, one that she harbors for the religiously significant time-span of seven years, is not that Dimmesdale is her lover but that Chillingworth is her husband.

Like Updike's Ruth and James's Maggie, Hawthorne's Hester is an artist trying to create order from a life broken by the impact of sex and guilt.[19] Like Ruth also (but unlike Maggie), Hester finds that matters of religious belief complicate her efforts. Both love men who believe in a traditional God, and both covet Maggie's bowl without the crack, but both question if their imaginations are vital enough to impose their visions—Hester's escape with Dimmesdale, Ruth's happy marriage to Jerry—on an unimaginative society. Maggie's artistic design may be easier to complete because her society values the necessity for superficial harmony above the claims of religious sensibility.

In all three cases, however, guilt prompts the artist. Art, sex, guilt, and religion are concerned with the inner life, with what James celebrated as the psychological level, and this equation may explain why Romance, Hawthorne's term for writing beyond the glare of verisimilitude, often begins with brooding about the guilt that emanates from erotic needs. Joel Porte even suggests—correctly, I think—that *The Scarlet Letter* can be read "as an allegory of art."[20] This is also why Updike prominently subtitles *Marry Me* "A Romance." Guilt acts not as a force of damnation but as a catalyst for inspiration. The artist's goal—Hester's, Maggie's, Ruth's—is to convince society to accept one's vision. To achieve that goal, to shape the realism of life into the Romance of desire, the three authors encourage their characters to avoid assigning blame. Indeed, Maggie quickly learns that to accuse her stepmother is to lose her husband. Hester and Ruth need not worry about pointing fingers because they themselves are adulteresses.

Thus sexual knowledge, whether with the blessing of the social contract or within the freedom of an adulterous affair, leads to both guilt and creativity. As voluptuous dark lady, as a literary cousin to Cooper's Cora, Hester gives and arouses passion. The A and Pearl proclaim her guilt to all those who remain within the safety of the community, but Hawthorne and the reader know that the letter and the child represent her artistic vision. This is why Pearl is described as both "a lovely and immortal flower" and "an imp of evil, emblem and product of sin." Hester is the successful artist. Her lover wastes away.

Dimmesdale's defeat is such a contrast that Updike speaks of the reader's "rejoicing" in the minister's fall.[21] The irony is that it could have been otherwise. He may return from the forest an adulterer, but he also reenters the community with a newfound eloquence that increases his power as a minister. Like Hester he learns that erotic freedom sparks creative instinct, but unlike her he uses his discovered potency to scrutinize only himself. Longing for Hester and even momentarily to ravish young girls, he rechannels his awakened energy to become a voyeur of the self. He is incapable of creating lasting art from his experience with adultery and guilt because he is too weak to imagine Maggie's bowl without the crack. The pain of anguish dominates the potential for art until his Election Day Sermon, but even then he gives way to the sin of pride.

Hester accepts the truth that Dimmesdale represses. When he asks if she has found peace, she smiles "drearily, looking down upon her bosom." On the exterior, of course, is the A, the emblem of both sin and passion. But beneath the surface are her breasts, the reality of passion alone and the flesh that the narrator of *The Blithedale Romance* turns from when he gazes at Zenobia. Her most urgent lesson for the minister is the famous declaration, "Preach! Write! Act! Do any thing, save to lie down and die!" [22] Immediately following her plea she frees her bosom of the A and her hair of the cap, as if another revelation of her sensuality might save him, but Dimmesdale cannot accommodate the dual demands of religious sensibility and erotic need. What for James is a legal and economic contract is for Hawthorne a moral commandment. Dimmesdale sees the stain on his chest as brighter than even the A on Hester's breast, and he sullies his Election Day Sermon—his final chance to create— with a prideful exclamation that he is not just a man suffering guilt but a prophet serving God. His "reputation of whitest sanctity" is a bogus creation, as Hawthorne makes quite clear when he immediately juxtaposes Hester "standing beside the scaffold of the pillory, with the scarlet letter still burning on her breast!" [23] With that little word *still* he underscores the enormity of Dimmesdale's failure to respond creatively to the complexity of adultery.

The relationships among sexual transgression, religion, and guilt are more explicit in *The Marble Faun*. Once, however, the reader evaluates the relatively obvious international theme begun by Hawthorne and perfected by James, and the eternally interesting question about the fortunate fall of man and whether active participation in sin is necessary to achieve the full measure of humanity, the reader would be justified in asking what Hawthorne's longest novel is about. R. W. B. Lewis's comment is instructive: "The novel's plot verges more than once on incoherence and wanders somewhat helplessly for about a dozen chapters, while we wonder whether Hawthorne will find the sustaining power to finish it. *The Marble*

Faun is not the best and probably not even the second-best of Hawthorne's novels; but its deficiencies are deficiencies of talent rather than of genius."[24] Lewis goes on to suggest that the theme is "the discovery of *time* as a metaphor of the experience of evil," and the reader recalls Emerson's observation in his great essay "Experience" that the fall of man is the discovery that he exists.

The Marble Faun may not be "even" Hawthorne's second-best novel, but it is surely his most puzzling. Man's meeting with time is crucial to the book, as is Porte's suggestion that the subject of *The Marble Faun* is the function of the artist.[25] Thus Donatello creates himself, showing that true art—as opposed to copying—must touch fallen humanity; Miriam personifies the artist confronted with shadows and mystery, illustrating the unity of art, violence, and sex; and Hilda represents the copyist, demonstrating the fear that self-expression is sinful. In all cases original art nudges the creator to doubt because legitimate creativity requires exposure of the inner life.

Indeed, Hilda's fear of the moral complexity of humanity is her primary obstacle to progressing from copying to creating. Equating sexual experience and its resulting knowledge of the self with negation, she apparently would choose death rather than violate her virginity. In this sense she is closer to Cooper's Alice or Stowe's little Eva than to the erotic heroines of Hawthorne, James, and Updike. It is as if she defines life as a trial to survive as stainlessly as possible, even to the extent of denying compassion to a suffering friend and walling herself up in a tower.

The puzzling quality of the novel is that Hawthorne approves of Hilda's sterility despite demonstrated sympathy with his earlier sensual women, Hester, Zenobia, and even the maturing Phoebe. Although his efforts are to the contrary, not the virginal Hilda but the mysterious Miriam is the most sympathetic character, for she is the one who carries the prominent Hawthornian stain. He declines to identify the source of the telling spot, but he directs every hint toward a sexual contact deemed illicit by law and commandment. As all readers know, the opposing reactions of Hilda and Miriam to Guido's portrait of Beatrice Cenci (who was raped by her father, whom she then plotted to kill) is crucial. Hilda responds negatively to the girl's plight, implying that the bloodstains of sex and revenge are defiling and insisting that Beatrice's fate is just: "Yes, yes; it was

terrible guilt, an inexpiable crime, and she feels it to be so. Therefore it is that the forlorn creature so longs to elude our eyes, and
forever vanish away into nothingness! Her doom is just." Miriam
reacts to Hilda's harshness from the point of view of a sexually experienced woman. Describing the painting, she identifies herself:
"Ah . . . if I could only get within her consciousness! . . . I would
give my life to know whether she thought herself innocent, or the
one great criminal since time began!" [26] In both reactions the nothingness of death in the presence of passion and art is an issue, but
where Hilda puritanically consigns the unfortunately initiated Beatrice to oblivion, Miriam humanely offers her own life to know the
secret of sex and guilt. Miriam's empathy with the "one great criminal" who may nevertheless be innocent reveals her own blemish and
reminds the reader of Hester and the most famous stain in American
literature.

Hilda's inability to accept Miriam's response as genuine, as the
kind of exposure of the self that a true creator must experience even
in the face of incest or adultery, persuades the reader that she is not
open to life. Yet Hawthorne, the other characters, and even Miriam
seem to excuse her denial of sympathy, and the result in *The Marble
Faun* is a curious split between Hawthorne's long-established association of creativity and sexual transgression and his unconvincing
effort to shy away from the equation in order to endorse the insipid
Hilda over the tragically experienced Miriam. This is not to suggest
that *The Marble Faun* would be a better novel without Hilda. Hilda
is necessary because she too is associated with Beatrice, but only in
the sense of innocence threatened with violation. An unnamed artist later sketches her as "Innocence, dying of a Blood-stain!" The
reader, however, looks to Miriam, who struggles not to die from but
to live with the stain. The allusion to Hilda's death from sex smacks
too much of Dimmesdale's failure to deal with the blot on his own
chest, and one finds oneself resisting Hawthorne's nudges in Hilda's
favor.

The most radical reaction to Hawthorne's favoritism for the Puritan copyist and to the novel as a whole may be Frederick Crews's.
In *The Sins of the Fathers: Hawthorne's Psychological Themes*,
Crews argues that to read *The Marble Faun* as a tale of regeneration
following the fall from primal innocence is to miss the point. The

religious trappings that intrigue Hawthorne (and Updike) are here unnecessary: "The theological speculations that his characters timidly raise and abandon are placed amid authorial comments that approach nihilism. . . . All life is seen in a backward glance from the brink of nothingness."[27] Rather than moral sensibility, writes Crews, weariness and despair are the keys to *The Marble Faun*. All of the author's former concerns are handled with what Crews calls "timid ambiguity." Despite the narrator's support and the characters' acquiesence, the reader cannot applaud Hilda's position that entrapment in the world's evil deserves no sympathy: "It should go without saying, by now, that when Hawthorne . . . takes extraordinary pains to emphasize the asexuality of a girl, he is preoccupied with the general sexuality of women."[28]

Hawthorne thus posits an analogy between sex and crime so that Hilda's witnessing the murder becomes a vicarious initiation into eroticism. The incessant reminders of catacombs, pits, and other pointed symbols indicate Hawthorne's great taboo: female sexuality. Establishing initiation into experience as a euphemism for sexual knowledge, he identifies passion as the most hideous of evils. Since Hawthorne is so repressed by prudishness in *The Marble Faun*, he cannot sustain the ironic distance from Kenyon that he manages with Holgrave and Coverdale. Thus his only recourse is spotless Hilda, with the unfortunate consequence that the symbolism of eroticism is often at odds with the narrator's commentary. The net result, says Crews in an astonishing conclusion, is "a smutty equivocation."[29]

The point here is not to examine Crews's interpretation but to illustrate how the intermingling of adultery, guilt, religion, and art in *The Marble Faun* affects qualified readers differently. Where Updike has fun with the intermingling in *A Month of Sundays* while simultaneously bowing to Hawthorne, Crews detects the infection of authorial anxiety about erotic imagery and adultery. His charge of "smutty equivocation" leaps from the page and stimulates the reader to rethink *The Marble Faun*. Significantly, Updike's comic homage to Hawthorne has suffered a similar blast. In an outraged dismissal of *A Month of Sundays*, Blanche Gelfant exhorts the reader to "be stern, take Updike seriously so that he might take himself more seriously and forgo the tricks of his trade—titillation, verbal pyrotechnics, philosophical chicanery, and factitious mushy theologizing. I think we must say No No to the obsessively repetitive sexual encounters, and No No to the obsessive naming of anatomical parts." [30] But I think we must say Yes because most of this has been a staple of American literature since Clara Wieland grabbed a knife to protect herself from her own brother, who had, after all, murdered his wife in his sister's bedroom while acting on what he thought were orders from God. Hawthorne disguises his concern with female sexuality and transgression by diverting the reader with statuary covered with "maiden-hair, and all sorts of verdant weed that thrive in the cracks and crevices of moist marble." [31] Updike may explicitly name "the anatomical parts," but the result in each novel is an unexpected and often disturbing insistence on the erotic underpinning of religious sensibility and spiritual contract.

Unlike James's Maggie, Hilda does not worry about specifically social obligations, but she does have the same general concern with breaking agreements. When, as a Protestant with Puritan beliefs, she seeks solace from the Roman Catholic confessional, she violates the terms of both religious doctrines. Curiously, Hawthorne applauds her transgressions, because following the confession he shows his heroine recovering from the stain that has soiled her innocence. Yet one does not forget the different sources of the blemish that marks both Hilda and Miriam. Erotic Miriam is implicated in the murder of the model who "blasted her sweet youth, and compelled her, as it were, to stain her womanhood with crime," while naïve Hilda wilts under the pressure of witnessing the event. [32] Hawthorne urges the reader to consider Hilda's bewilderment as seriously as Miriam's suffering, but the reader balks because he does not accept the veiled suggestions that knowledge via sexual transgression is tantamount to evil. Hilda is forever shrinking from the complications of humanity, as when she responds to a question about the natural—as opposed to the human—freedom indicated in the statue of the Praxiteles Faun: "It perplexes me . . . neither do I quite like to think about it." The contrast with Miriam is startling: "Miriam had great apparent freedom of intercourse; her manners were so far from evincing shyness, that it seemed easy to become acquainted with her, and not difficult to develope a casual acquaintance into intimacy." [33] Refraining from identifying the extent of the "intercourse" or the nature of the "intimacy," Hawthorne dodges in his last novel what he specifies in his first: that adultery can stimulate creativity. Thus the harmony that Hilda finds in the confessional is as superficial as that at the conclusion of *The Golden Bowl*, but with this crucial distinction: James's characters acknowledge the superficiality and yet observe the harmony for the good of the social contract, while Hawthorne's characters confuse the superficiality with the fundamentally positive. Hilda's stain is inconsequential beside Hester's A and Maggie's cracked bowl.

Miriam, however, stands squarely with her fictional kinswomen in nurturing the promise of erotic intensity. She has no little Pearl to indicate the extent of her experience, but she understands her affinity with the meaning of the crimson A. The sexual implications are unmistakable in her comment to Kenyon: "'My secret is not a pearl. . . . Yet a man might drown himself in plunging after it!' . . . It is no precious pearl, as I just now told him; but my dark-red carbuncle—red as blood."[34] Thus Hawthorne is of two minds in *The Marble Faun*. He hopes to celebrate Puritan America's attitude toward the moral contract against the European attitude toward art, but he is undecided about the necessity of sexual experience for generating creativity. The result is that he recommends the beauty of Roman art, represented by Miriam, at the same time that he praises the purity of American copies, represented by Hilda. The red of Hester's letter and the white of her daughter's name, unified in *The Scarlet Letter*, are forever separated in *The Marble Faun*.

Updike's transgressors long for a similar unity. Just as perplexed as Hawthorne's characters by the tension between sexual desire and religious belief, they follow paths of experience already mapped by Hester, Dimmesdale, and Miriam. Hester knows the forest, Miriam the catacombs, and Marshfield the desert, and thus all three suffer an expulsion of sorts while pursuing the promise of erotic delight. Yet the ambiguities of religious faith are an issue of equal importance to them. Faced with concern for their spirits while acknowledging the demands of their bodies, they are familiar with the chasm of despair. Hawthorne may insist on the separation of the material and the impalpable while Updike suggests otherwise, but the latter's essays and novels show that he learned well the lessons of his New England forerunner as he adapted them to his own needs.

NOTES

1. John Updike, "Creatures of the Air," *Assorted Prose* (New York: Knopf, 1965) 307.

2. John Updike, *Picked-Up Pieces* (New York: Knopf, 1975) 378, 173.

3. John Updike, "An Introduction to Nabokov's Lectures," *Hugging the Shore* (New York: Knopf, 1983) 236. This essay was originally published in Vladimir Nabokov, *Lectures on Literature*, ed. Fredson Bowers (New York: Harcourt Brace Jovanovich/Bruccoli Clark, 1980).

4. *Picked-Up Pieces* 327, 507.

5. John Updike, "Melville's Withdrawal," *Hugging the Shore* 83.

6. *Hugging the Shore* 90, 91.

7. *Hugging the Shore* 295.

8. *Hugging the Shore* 73, 74, 75.

9. *Hugging the Shore* 76.

10. *Hugging the Shore* 76.

11. John Updike, *A Month of Sundays* (New York: Knopf, 1975) 48–49.

12. *A Month of Sundays* 51–52.

13. *Hugging the Shore* 77.

14. *Hugging the Shore* 77.

15. *Hugging the Shore* 77–78.

16. *Hugging the Shore* 78.

17. *Hugging the Shore* 80.

18. Nathaniel Hawthorne, *The Scarlet Letter* (Columbus: Ohio State University Press, 1962) 164. See Jerome Klinkowitz, "Hawthorne's Sense of an Ending," *The Practice of Fiction in America* (Ames: Iowa State University Press, 1980).

19. See Catherine Cox Wessel, "Strategies for Survival in James's *The Golden Bowl*," *American Literature* 55 (1983): 587: "Maggie finds herself in the fortunate position of a superiorly gifted artist."

20. Joel Porte, *The Romance in America* (Middletown, Conn.: Wesleyan University Press, 1969) 99.

21. *Hugging the Shore* 76.

22. *The Scarlet Letter* 191, 198.

23. *The Scarlet Letter* 249, 250.

24. R. W. B. Lewis, *The American Adam: Innocence, Tragedy, and Tradition in the Nineteenth Century* (1955; Chicago: University of Chicago Press, 1964) 121.

25. Porte 137–51.

26. Nathaniel Hawthorne, *The Marble Faun: Or, The Romance of Monte Beni* (Columbus: Ohio State University Press, 1968) 66–67.

27. Frederick Crews, *The Sins of the Fathers: Hawthorne's Psychological Themes* (New York: Oxford University Press, 1970) 214.

28. Crews 217.

29. Crews 225.

30. Blanche H. Gelfant, "Fiction Chronicle," *Hudson Review* 28 (1975): 313.

31. *The Marble Faun* 38.

32. *The Marble Faun* 190.

33. *The Marble Faun* 13, 21.

34. *The Marble Faun* 130.

Part Two   # The Novels

Adultery and   3
The Golden Bowl

He thought of Mrs Holme's compatriot Henry James at the
moment of its dawning on him that *The Golden Bowl*, say,
was to be a work of some complexity.[1]
　　　　　　　　　　　—Michael Innes, *Money from Holme*

his epigraph, taken from Michael Innes's spoof of the
crime thriller, is cited not to indicate a flippant attitude toward Henry James's last novel but to suggest
the wide-ranging reputation for ambiguity and complexity that it
continues to enjoy. More than eighty years have passed since James
published *The Golden Bowl* in 1904, but it challenges qualified
readers today as urgently as when it first appeared. Not only the
density of its prose but also the intricacy of its dissection of the relationships among sexual transgression, knowledge, and domestic
economics puzzles the reader unprepared to offer what James calls
"attention of perusal." *The Golden Bowl* is *the* novel of adultery in
American literature.

Like Hawthorne's *The Marble Faun* and Updike's *Couples* and
Marry Me, *The Golden Bowl* concerns the meeting of sexual knowledge and innocence, but unlike Hilda or Updike's heroines, Maggie
Verver turns the confrontation with illicit sexuality into experience
and emerges triumphant.[2] The issue that intrigues the reader is the
cost of her victory. The parallel with Hawthorne is instructive.
Hawthorne's praise of Hilda's asexuality is forced, but he supplies
enough information for the reader to understand that Miriam's sensuality is likewise an attractive though dark quality. One is never
quite sure where Hawthorne stands in the relationship between
sexuality and knowledge, and one senses, in the *The Marble Faun* at
least, a tension between his eagerness to explore the pits and catacombs of sex and his reluctance to probe too far. The James of the

major phase is not so hesitant. Yet to point to his unblinking examination of adultery in *The Golden Bowl* is not to suggest that the matter is uncontroversial.

I

A survey of the criticism shows that many influential critics question the moral value of the late James, as when F. R. Leavis in *The Great Tradition* criticizes *The Golden Bowl* because, he argues, James permits his concern for "technical elaboration" to overwhelm his sense of life and his moral judgment. This opinion is unfortunate because it both overlooks James's position as an early modernist interested, as modernists invariably were, with such aesthetic matters as form and pattern, and neglects the ironic relationship between Maggie's ignorance of social forms and James's understanding of novelistic patterns. In both cases, heroine and author, moral value is assigned to the appreciation of form.

Sallie Sears is the most perceptive commentator on this point, and her defense of the novel against its negative critics is pertinent: "The critical reaction to *The Golden Bowl*—preponderantly negative—comes from a reluctance, almost phobic in nature, not only to grant the artist his premises but even to see what they are to begin with. *The Golden Bowl* is radical, extreme, modern. It persistently has been judged by standards irrelevant not only to itself but to modern art in general and, in significant ways, all art." Sears defines the vision of the novel as "rapacious as any nightmare of Dreiser's," and she finds in it "ravage and woe and brutality."[3] Cruelty and exploitation, both economic and sexual, are ineradicable qualities of humanity, and Maggie must first accept and then act upon what her husband already knows: that everything is "terrible in the heart of man." If she is to succeed, if she is to transform adultery into creativity, she must dodge the temptation that besets the many characters of Hawthorne who scrub at their stains in an effort to have beauty without birthmarks. This is why Maggie can mature to an understanding which James approves of but which disturbs his skeptical critics: that everyone is culpable including, perhaps most of all, Maggie herself. Difficult as it is, she has to admit that while moral principles should rest at the center of social forms, morals are not easily judged. It is as if she is halfway to Updike's insistence in *Rabbit, Run* and *A Month of Sundays* that not ethics but belief is the issue. James is not interested in the religious sensibility that attracts Updike, but both authors know that sympathy for wayward individuals must be offered far beyond the simplistic pieties of right and wrong.

Sears's wonderful description of Maggie as a "Milly Theale who does not turn her face to the wall" and as one whose "ruthlessness is masked by conscious piety" suggests a Maggie more demonic than I am willing to concede, but it also indicates the range of responses that the novel encourages.[4] James sets up the sexual transgression so that while Maggie justifies the fight for the Prince in terms of love, the reader knows that romance is kin to brutality. It may be desirable that Maggie triumphs, but victory over Charlotte does not make her any less culpable. This vision of a pluralistic morality frustrates readers who require a traditional accounting of good and bad.

Sears describes *The Golden Bowl* as a novel in which "'good' and 'evil' become so radically juxtaposed that all distinction between them crumbles, which is to say that as categories they cease to exist."[5] The point is well taken, for it warns the reader away from superficial judgments of morality and directs him to James's position that moral fiction must be evaluated in terms of the felt life the author evokes rather than in terms of the indecencies he exposes. James argued this opinion in his essay "The Art of Fiction" published twenty years before *The Golden Bowl*:

> There is one point at which the moral sense and the artistic sense lie very near together; that is in the light of the very obvious truth that the deepest quality of a work of art will always be the quality of the mind of the producer. In proportion as that intelligence is fine will the novel, the picture, the statue partake of the substance of beauty and truth. . . . No good novel will ever proceed from a superficial mind.[6]

Mediocre performances, implies James, are immoral. Notions of right and wrong are not the issue.

Yet it is because they are not the issue that some readers complain about ambiguity. If adultery and transgression are at stake, the argument goes, then condemnation and blame must be forthcoming; the

reader needs to know where the author stands. One gives thanks
that James resists such pressure. Ambiguity may be encouraged, but
John Bayley has a point when he argues that the moral vision of *The
Golden Bowl* is not the cause of confusion: "The results he achieves
are only ambiguous if we are determined to view them from the
standpoint of 'moral values,' rather than from the standpoint of personality and what James makes of it." Bayley suggests to the negative critics that James approaches *The Golden Bowl* not from the
pinnacle of a moral position but from his fascination with an interesting character: "the lesson of how to embrace and inhabit a character without making it either a projection of the author's self or a
vessel of moral discernment."[7] This is why Maggie, the Prince, and
Charlotte have what Bayley calls "so much more of the gusto of
creation," so much more solidity than Isabel Archer, who is shaped
too much by James's idea of her destiny. Form and character, not
right and wrong, determine moral value.

R. B. J. Wilson concurs in a statement that should be quoted
in full:

> If "attention of perusal" . . . does in fact reveal that he evolved dur-
> ing the Lamb House years a form of literary discourse affording em-
> pathetic understanding without permitting sentimental sympathy
> for, or exclusive identification with, any one character but relating,
> rather, all characters to human and moral absolutes without allowing
> those absolutes any didactic force, then he has clearly extended the
> frontiers of fiction. The provisions within the text of this novel testify
> to his having depicted the moral consciousness in ways that free that
> depiction from the moral simplifications that always threaten and
> sometimes overwhelm narrative, especially when it is in the third
> person. . . . Denied omniscient explanations, confronted instead
> from point to point with the same vantage point shared by the author
> whose voice is constantly with him, the reader must deliberate on
> ambivalences within the given appearance of each figure and eschew
> moral judgment for moral cogitation.[8]

Cogitation, not judgment; ambiguous characters, not moral certainty: James explained one focus of his novel in the 1909 preface,
but many readers still refuse to listen: "We see very few persons in
'The Golden Bowl,' but the scheme of the book, to make up for that,
is that we shall really see about as much of them as a coherent liter-

ary form permits." Complex characterization negates moral sim-
plification. If all the characters are guilty in one way or another,
then ambiguity of appearance is not confusion of sense. The careful
reader does figure out what is happening.

What one finally discovers in *The Golden Bowl* is that the pressure of economics joins the enticement of sex and the responsibility
of knowledge to depict a marital atmosphere in which the extremes
of right and wrong are blurred. Sexual transgression threatens more
than the sanctity of the bedroom; it also leads to violation of contract in ways that Hawthorne and Updike do not consider, and the
unhappy result is that the harmony of society cracks under the burden of domestic particulars. James's notebooks, letters, and earlier
fiction show that he was concerned with these complexities long before he completed *The Golden Bowl*.

The primary complication, he knew, was adultery. As early as 3
November 1894, while musing in his notebooks about the material
that was to become *The Wings of the Dove*, he touched on the challenge of writing about English—as opposed to French—adultery:

> If I were writing for a French public the whole thing would be
> simple—the elder, the "other," woman would simply be the mistress
> of the young man, and it would be a question of his taking on the
> dying girl for a time—having a temporary liaison with her. But one
> can do so little with English adultery—it is so much less inevitable,
> and so much more ugly in all its hiding and lying side. It is so under-
> mined by our immemorial tradition of original freedom of choice, and
> by our practically universal acceptance of divorce.[9]

Hiding and lying and ugliness—he had written about this very side
of adultery in the 1888 novella "A London Life," which I shall discuss later, but for now it is important to understand the difficulty
that the subject of adultery posed for a late-Victorian author in England or America. Hawthorne, for example, relegates the crucial
meeting of Hester and Dimmesdale to a hidden moment in the forest nine months before *The Scarlet Letter* begins. Little Pearl may
be the public evidence of sexual transgression, but Hawthorne cannot discuss the private affair.

James, however, was more fascinated by the nuances of the social
whirl than Hawthorne, and he knew that the snake lurked in the

drawing room as well as in the forest. The problem was how to depict the reality of transgression. In his notebook for 14 February 1895, for instance, he writes of trying to come up with material for a "short 'International' novel that Harpers want," recalls an earlier journal entry about a social complication that would later become *The Golden Bowl*, and finally suggests that the subject of adultery may not be suitable for American readers of magazines: "*Everything* about it qualifies it for *Harper* except the subject—or rather, I mean, except the adulterine element *in* the subject. But may it not be simply a question of *handling* that? For God's sake let me try: I want to plunge into it." [10] But plunge he could not do, at least not into a tale of adultery for journal readers. As much as nine years later, still thinking about the sexual betrayal at the heart of *The Golden Bowl*, he wrote to William Dean Howells (8 January 1904) that his latest novel "isn't, alas, so employable" for serialization. [11]

Sexual transgression may not be acceptable fare for magazine readers, but it could be developed for those who buy novels. As all Jamesians know, James had been thinking about *The Golden Bowl* for a long time, even to the extent of outlining its complexities nearly twelve years before the novel was published. Part of his notebook entry for 28 November 1892 reads:

> Situation, not closely connected with the above, suggested by something lately told one about a simultaneous marriage, in Paris . . . of a father and a daughter—an only daughter. The daughter—American of course—is engaged to a young Englishman, and the father, a widower and still youngish, has sought in marriage at exactly the same time an American girl of very much the same age as his daughter. Say he has done it to console himself in his abandonment—to make up for the loss of the daughter, to whom he has been devoted. I see a little tale, *n'est-ce pas?*—in the idea that they all shall have married, as arranged, with this characteristic consequence—that the daughter fails to hold the affections of the young English husband, whose approximate mother-in-law the pretty young wife of the father will now have become. [12]

Two phrases in the outline strike the reader. First, the daughter is "American of course" and thus in the sophisticated English world of Jamesian domesticity is unable initially to cope with the complexities of adultery practiced by those who define morality as "high

intelligence." Second, the situation has the "characteristic consequence" that sexual transgression is bound to occur when an innocent American girl, devoted to her father, marries an experienced
English man, devoted to his pleasure. Latent incest frames hidden,
ugly, lying adultery; no wonder James could not develop the tale for
Harper's.

But he did develop the novel, spending thirteen months on it and
exposing the very thing that Updike took as his own subject matter
many years later: the terror beneath the mundane, the fear that
looms beyond the compromises and complacencies of the daily routine. Indeed, Leon Edel insists that the fearful domestic relationships in *The Golden Bowl* begin with James's own family life.
Finding in the Prince-Adam-Charlotte triangle the enigma of father-
mother-aunt with which James had to contend as a child, Edel argues that like Maggie the young Henry became confused about his
relationship with each. James's working out of Maggie's predicament
thus allows him to resolve an old domestic puzzle and to complete,
for the first time in his twenty novels, the maturation of a female
character. Edel also suggests that the crack in the bowl stands for
the flaw in James's life, especially when he realized in old age that he
had lived too exclusively with art and not enough with experience.
Thus, in insisting on the primacy of love in *The Golden Bowl*,
James, says Edel, was reflecting the new presence in his life of "the
fun-loving Jocelyn Persse, whom James adored." [13]

Whatever the case, the biographical connection urged by Edel or
the "adulterine element" defined by James, *The Golden Bowl* all
but reduces society to a charmed circle protected by immense
wealth. The charm degenerates first to insulation and then to blindness about motive and self. Yet James's interest is in not only how
adultery wrecks the circle but also how the snake is expelled from
the drawing room. Maggie learns to redirect the boat—a central
metaphor in the novel—without rocking it; if she rocks too publicly,
people might drown. Society, despite its flaws and illusions—its
cracks—assures equilibrium and even decency; and the tarnished
triumph of love over adultery, even at the cost of lies and deceit, is
crucial to the well-being of social discourse.

The problems of sex and guilt intrigued James for much of his career. Not only his notebooks but also some of his earlier, less well

known fiction reveals his fascination with the attraction of adultery and its impact on social harmony. Of all nineteenth-century American novelists, he understood best that marriage is more contract than sacrament and that contracts are written to be broken. How does society remain civilized, then, when its signed agreements publicly break down? In the 1888 novella "A London Life," James asks a similar question. The American Laura Wing moves through the tale on a dry run for the far more complex Maggie. Although a sister rather than a husband is the adulterer in "A London Life," one might be dipping into the pages of *The Golden Bowl* when reading this description of Laura: "A year ago she knew nothing, and now she knew almost everything; and the worst of her knowledge (or at least the worst of the fears she had raised upon it) had come to her in that beautiful place, where everything was so full of peace and purity."[14] One thinks of Maggie waiting for the Prince to return from his weekend with Charlotte and realizing that nothing is full of peace and purity. The serpent is in the garden, and Laura, like Maggie, must confront the slithering insinuations of adultery. Her sister Selina's infidelities are bad enough, but public revelation of them would be catastrophic.

Like Fanny Assingham and her original, mistaken assessment of Maggie, Selina believes that Laura "seemed born for innocence." And even Laura herself, again like Maggie, sees that "she wanted rather to be taught a certain fortitude—how to live and hold up one's head even while knowing that things were very bad." As an old English friend says to her, "You Americans have such a lot of false delicacy. . . . This isn't a crying country."[15] One recalls James's notebook entry made four years later when he first began thinking about the character that would become Maggie: "American of course."

The innocent Maggie must accept what Laura senses but reacts against: "the same curious duplicity. . . . that perfection of machinery which can still at certain times make English life go on of itself with a stately rhythm long after there is corruption within it." This is a classic definition of James's understanding of the necessary superficial harmony, and it suggests his most crucial variation on the theme of adultery, guilt, and belief begun by Hawthorne and extended by Updike. Despite these similarities between the novella

and the novel, however, Maggie rarely appears in the light that
James flashes on Laura: "that she was a weak, inconsequent, spas-
modic young person, with a standard not really, or at any rate not
continuously, high."[16] Maggie's standard, needless to say, is continuously high. She learns to act on what Laura rejects.

The problem is how to interpret James's position in this tale of the
"adulterine element," for a reading of "A London Life" can affect
(though not direct) one's understanding of *The Golden Bowl*. Edel's
introduction to volume 7 of *The Complete Tales* has initiated a dis-
pute about James's changing view of adultery, and Heath Moon, for
one, dismisses Edel's comments as a "totally misguided reading."

According to Edel, James began "A London Life" during his so-
journ in Tuscany and Venetia in 1886–87. There James heard a story
about the suicide of a young Frenchwoman upon discovering that
her mother had lovers. As Edel points out, "The predicament of a
girl in an acute state of anxiety seems to have had a particular appeal
to Henry James as a dramatic subject." In "A London Life," James
develops the girl's anxiety from the adulteries and likely divorce of
an older sister who is an American married into English society.
Edel insists that the novella reveals James "finally recognising that
the world of 'society' is not as rigid as he had believed: that social indiscretions are sometimes committed without tragic consequences"; and that the puritanical Laura exaggerates the evils of the
sister's transgressions. Years later, writes Edel, James wondered why
he had made Laura an American when nationality did not matter in
"A London Life" as it did in "Daisy Miller": "London society provided adulterous subjects in abundance. What had mattered was
the puritanical stiffness of the girl, her 'wild, vague, frantic, gesture.'"[17] If Edel is correct, then adultery does not pose a serious
threat to contract and harmony in the late James.

Heath Moon disagrees. Quoting from James's preface to the volume in the New York Edition that includes "A London Life," Moon
argues that Edel's interpretation has replaced James's intentions as
expressed in that preface. If, Moon asks, James describes Laura as a
heroine of "acuteness and intensity, reflexion and passion" who is
also "touching," "rare," "charming," and "decent," how can one
credit Edel's description of her as mistaken to be distressed by her
sister's adulteries and as an illustration of James's newfound sense of

82

The Novels

"taking an indulgent, though not altogether approving, view of the laxity of the married American woman and a critical view of the inflexible morality of her sister?"[18] Moon's query makes it difficult to accept Edel's point that the James of the late 1880s finally recognized how social indiscretions of a sexual nature did not inevitably produce serious consequences. One should also add that if this were true, James would hardly have offered the selfish, shallow, and hypocritical Selina as an adulteress who should be treated sympathetically. Selina is a far cry from Charlotte Stant.

This challenge to Edel's newly indulgent James is persuasive, and it has consequences for readers who are puzzled by Maggie's harsh treatment of Charlotte. If, their argument runs, James no longer judges adultery to have disastrous social results, then he cannot support Laura's and Maggie's outraged reactions to transgression. But this line of thought is mistaken. Citing the notebooks, in which James describes his plans to make the wayward Selina "easily depraved," "frivolous," and a "shallow *pretending* cat," and the preface in which James refers to the "wicked woman of my story," Moon suggests that the brazenly self-righteous Selina has cast a spell over Edel.

One doubts if Edel is that gullible, but one notes that Charlotte Stant weaves a similar spell of her own and that the latest in a long line of commentators to fall for it is Gore Vidal. Although Vidal seems wrong in pointing to a specific change in James after 1880, he does describe James's interest in domestic intrigue with his usual wit: "For him, the novel must now be something other than the faithful detailing of familiar types engaged in mating rituals against carefully noted backgrounds." Vidal—mistakenly I think—joins those who reserve most of their sympathy for the adulterers: "This means that the woman must always be made to suffer for sexual transgression while the man suffers not at all or, in the case of the Prince, very little—although the renewed and intensified closeness to Maggie may well be a rarefied punishment."[19] He goes on to call Maggie and her father "monsters on a divine scale." Witty but wrong, this opinion ignores the social and historical context in which James wrote "A London Life" in 1886–87 and began taking notes for *The Golden Bowl* in 1892.

Biographical evidence shows that James was fascinated by the revelations of sexual misconduct that shook the higher reaches of Lon-

don society during the widely publicized divorce trials of summer
and fall, 1886. Calling the scandal that engulfed Sir Charles Dilke
"the worse divorce trial to rock the English upper classes since the
enactment of the Matrimonial Causes Act of 1857," Moon reminds
the reader that the Dilke hearing was shortly followed by Lord Colin
Campbell's petition for divorce, which publicized sexual transgressions of larger proportion than anything in the Dilke case. "A London
Life" registers the aftershock of this now forgotten but then renowned trial, and it is not likely that James would have judged such
sexual lawlessness with indulgence. Moon calls attention to a letter to
Charles Eliot Norton in which James speaks of the "hideous" divorce
case that will "besmirch exceedingly the already very damaged pres-
tige of the English upper class." [20] The instability of domestic particulars in high places clearly concerned James. Laura's indignation at the
casualness of upper-class adultery may be overbearingly judgmental,
but it is also an expression of disillusion at the public exposure of
wanton behavior. Sexual betrayal, in short, threatens what to her
imagination is high civilization. Selfish absorption in sensual pleasure renders the rhythms of the social contract discordant. Public
revelation and divorce follow, the superficial harmony cracks, and
one nears the complexity of Maggie's dilemma in *The Golden Bowl*.

As James worked his way toward his greatest novel from dry run
to notebook entries to draft to final product, and as he pondered
Maggie's predicament in light of the public scandal of the London
divorce trials, he was persuaded that *The Golden Bowl* would be a
masterpiece. His correspondence suggests his delight. In a well-
known letter (20 May 1904) to his literary agent, J. B. Pinker, he
writes: ". . . am producing the best book, I seem to conceive, that I
have ever done. I have really done it fast, for what it is, and for the
way I do it—*the* way I seem condemned to; which is to *overtreat*
my subject by developments and amplifications that have, in large
part, eventually to be greatly compressed, but to the prior opera-
tion of which the thing afterwards owes what is most durable in its
quality." Now note his exultation: "I have written, in perfection,
200,000 words of the G.B.—with the rarest perfection!" [21] Other
letters indicate his pleasure at the reception of *The Golden Bowl*. In
a correspondence (18 February 1905) to Edmund Gosse he under-
states the joy: "The thing has 'done' much less ill here [United

States] than anything I have ever produced," and in a letter (21 February 1905) to Mrs. W. K. Clifford he expresses his pleasure directly: "*The Golden Bowl* is in its *fourth* edition—unprecedented!"[22]

Yet not all his epistolary responses reveal such joy. *The Golden Bowl* is a difficult novel, and especially interesting is a reply (23 November 1905) to his brother William's mystification: "I mean (in response to what you write me of your having read the *Golden B.*) to try to produce some uncanny form of thing, in fiction, that will gratify you, as Brother—but let me say, dear William, that I shall greatly be humiliated if you *do* like it, and thereby lump it, in your affection, with things, of the current age, that I have heard you express admiration for and that I would sooner descend to a dishonored grave than have written."[23] Although the humor of James's exasperation strikes the reader at once, so too does the confidence with which he defends his last novel against the doubtful standard of "things" of the current age.

II

In a very real sense *The Golden Bowl* exposes that age as it teeters on the brink of loss of harmony. At the end of the novel James admits that the harmony lacks depth, but he also understands its necessity because it encompasses domestic economics, love and knowledge, and sexual attraction. His narrator already knows what has taken Maggie a long novel to discover: that one does not run to the London divorce courts, that one does not brand the transgressors with a scarlet A, and that one accepts a compromise which "was n't less sustained for being superficial."[24]

To illustrate the union of necessity and superficiality, James reduces society to two marriages and sanctions the institution of wedlock while he simultaneously challenges its conventions. In this sense *The Golden Bowl* fits Tony Tanner's definition of the bourgeois novel as taking marriage for its subject while constantly exposing its flaws; but, one recalls, Tanner does not consider *The Golden Bowl* a true bourgeois fiction because it is too much a "novel of metaphor." This definition seems too limiting. James clearly shows that with its combination of pitfalls and promises marriage in his final novel is a metaphor for society itself. The crack in the bowl, in the marriages, and in the social contract is potentially devastating, but it can be covered with gilt so long as the blemish is acknowledged. Flaws are understandable but blindness is inexcusable. This is a long way from Hester Prynne's iron men and their opinions.

Artificially arranged forms, business as well as familial contracts, shape both society and marriage, and thus all becomes monstrous— what the Prince calls "terrible in the heart of man"—if the defects of acquisitiveness, adultery, and naïve innocence are permitted to distort the delicate order. James's social arrangements are not only aesthetic and moral but economic as well, and it is because of this latter emphasis that his fiction of sex and guilt differs from that of Hawthorne and Updike. Love for him is both ceremony and contract. It is significant, for example, that the two weddings in *The Golden Bowl* largely result from business considerations. One does not forget the first paragraph of the novel with its description of the Prince strolling through "his" London. Note the emphasis on tribute, gold, and loot: "Brought up on the legend of the City to which the world paid tribute, he recognised in the present London much more than in contemporary Rome the real dimensions of such a case. . . . he had strayed simply enough into Bond Street, where his imagination, working at comparatively short range, caused him now and then to stop before a window in which objects massive and lumpish, in silver and gold . . . were as tumbled together as if, in the insolence of the Empire, they had been the loot of far-off victories" (1:3). The irony soon becomes apparent, for at that very moment the Prince is being bought by Adam Verver's lawyers. He himself is the loot, the crowning acquisition to Verver's "rifling" of the Golden Isles.

Passion and love may follow, but business leads the way. Later, Verver's proposal to Charlotte after inviting her to join him while he negotiates a price for the Damascene tiles recalls the Prince's contrasting inability to purchase anything of value when window-shopping on Bond Street, waiting for the attorneys to notarize his marriage to Verver's daughter. In both cases Adam controls the checkbook and thus the arrangements. Charlotte and the Prince are as they were in the Bloomsbury shop, ostensibly buying a present for Maggie, the one trying to offer an inexpensive, flawed gift, the other determined not to accept. James does not hide Charlotte's meaning: "You may think of me what you will, but I don't care. . . . I came back for this. . . . To have one hour alone with you" (1:89). Sexual consummation is as much currency exchanged as passion indulged. The Prince readily understands the connections, just as he knows that Adam has relieved him of "all anxiety about his married life in the same manner in which he relieved him on the score of his bank-account" (1:292). In other words, Verver has not only purchased the Prince but usurped his position. The strange attraction between father and daughter has, Amerigo muses, "the same deep intimacy of the commercial," and after the two marriages the Prince and Charlotte suffer what she calls lives of "debased" currency.

Laurence Holland quite rightly points out that the passion between the adulterers would be judged illicit by the very society that encourages it, and yet their affair has a dignity that is clarified by the contrast with the casual adultery of Lady Castledean and Mr. Blint.[25] Still, the Prince and Charlotte's intimacy and Maggie and Adam's relationship are wrong to the extent of perverting the natural order. Someone has to fix the crack by rebuilding the bowl, to coax a marriage of form and substance from the perverted order, and this Maggie does when she accepts the unstated mandate to action.

One of the subtleties of James's plan is the way Maggie acts while appearing to the other characters to languish. Choosing indirect pressure instead of overt demonstration, she hides her initial jealousy by manipulating the marriages in order to restore the bowl's surface and to reshape the contracts. She must, in other words, stare behind Arthur Gordon Pym's white veil (the Prince remembers Poe's novel from his childhood). When she does so, she witnesses a horror that had seemed to be beyond her imagination:

> She saw at all events why horror itself had almost failed her; the horror that, foreshadowed in advance, would by her thought have made everything that was unaccustomed in her cry out with pain; the horror of finding evil seated all at its ease where she had only dreamed of good; the horror of the thing hideously *behind*, behind so much trusted, so much pretended, nobleness, cleverness, tenderness. It was the first sharp falsity she had known in her life. (2:237)

Later realizing the enormity of her love for the Prince and the ineffectiveness of her jealousy of Charlotte, she defines her understanding of permanent love as that which transcends jealousy: "My idea is this, that when you only love a little you're naturally not jealous—or are only jealous also a little, so that it does n't matter. But when you love in a deeper and intenser way, then you're in the very same proportion jealous; your jealousy has intensity and, no doubt, ferocity. When however you love in the most abysmal and unutterable way of all—why then you're beyond everything, and nothing can pull you down" (2:262). If she permits her natural jealousy to limit her to the first two degrees of love, she will challenge the Prince's sense of being a "grand man" and thereby lose him. Thus she must reject the lure of the "rights of resentment" and inch her way toward a renegotiation of the broken contract. Most of all Maggie must give up her pleasure in manipulating her husband and his mistress, in enjoying the "sweetness" of her "sense of possession," and in feeling the "sharpest thrill" in the way she has the Prince "straitened and tied" (2:20, 192).

Slowly and subtly developing Maggie's growing awareness of the need to act against the horror of the "thing hideously behind," James inadvertently initiates a long-standing critical debate about Maggie's motive and methods. This is not the place to discuss the complexities of the disagreement, but the highlights are relevant. As with one's interpretation of Laura's reaction in "A London Life," so one's reading of Maggie's determination to repair both contract and ceremony affects one's understanding of the novel.

Walter Wright points out that as early as 1907 Oliver Elton argued that the reader finally rejects Maggie to sympathize with Charlotte. Joseph Firebaugh is more direct; he calls Maggie a "heartless Machiavellian absolutest" obsessed with preserving a "false world of appearances to conceal the truth about her life." Finally, Sallie Sears judges Maggie harshly: "Her personality represents a union of what always were for James the destructive traits of the soul. . . . She loses the innocence, the freshness, the genuine humility that were her angelic if less potent virtues and becomes a receptacle for will alone." Although her compassion for Charlotte is legitimate, she punishes the adulterers beyond the limits of their crime.[26]

Sears's opinion is especially instructive because of her vocabulary of "innocence," "freshness," "humility," and "angelic." It is as if Maggie should remain forever in the garden, as much a literary cousin to Hawthorne's Hilda as her loss of virginity in marriage will permit, and never to join Hester and Miriam at the edge of the forest, staring at the thing behind. Holland has something like this in mind when he praises Maggie for "redeeming" the marriages, and Dorothea Krook explicitly defines *The Golden Bowl* as a "great fable . . . of the redemption of man by the transforming power of human love."[27] Both opinions—that which damns Maggie to the depths of outraged avenger and that which elevates her to the pinnacle of redeeming angel—strike me as too extreme. The one makes her a vindictive Othello, pulling down the world with her jealousy; the other makes her a forgiving Milly Theale, converting the world with her love. It seems to me that for his last great heroine James combines elements of Milly Theale's love and Kate Croy's hardness to create a character who can walk out of the garden of her father's protection without stumbling in the forest of her husband's adultery. It is as if James remembered Hawthorne's Hilda and Miriam and united them.

Maggie sweeps into action and learns that she must pity those who have betrayed her even while she punishes them. If she is to reestablish the economic contract and rededicate the marriage sacrament, she must indulge in lies even to the extent of creating a bowl without the flaw. The key difference between intimacy with her father and passion with her husband is that with the latter she is finally aware of the crack. The cost is high—leaving Adam and forcing Charlotte to play the role of banished adulteress—but the victory is worth the price. One of James's ironies is that to urge the truth she has to forge the lie, at least a public lie that the adultery never takes place. No London divorce court for her. Only thus can she readjust the relationship of money and love. Lying to Charlotte during the card game at Fawns, insisting that she accuses Charlotte of "nothing," Maggie agrees to a "conscious perjury" with the sexual transgressor who is her childhood friend, her father's wife, and her husband's mistress. Their embrace on the terrace smacks more of a Judas betrayal than an angelic redemption, and their ensuing kiss is described as "prodigious" (2:250, 251).

James insists on the necessity of the perjury, for Maggie learns that harmony is better than denunciation. When, at the end, she brings the first volume of a novel to Charlotte, she offers it with a typical Jamesian irony: "*This* is the beginning" (2:311). Her final sacrifice to the new beginning of her marriage is her willingness to accept Charlotte's accusation that she has always loathed the union of her father and stepmother. Thus leaving Charlotte her pride, Maggie acts on the Prince's truth that terror resides everywhere.

For Hawthorne the terror refers to the violation of the sanctity of the human heart; for Updike it suggests an absence of grace in all its manifestations, the fluidity that his characters always lose and continually seek. For James the terror is more social and thus more general, and it includes the awesome responsibility of knowledge. To live in the world one must know the proverbial tree. John Bayley asks a key question: Are loving and knowing, two ideas that form a complex pattern in James's fiction, opposed to each other or closely related? His answer is succinct: knowledge "provides a scale of value, intimately pondered by James, against which to measure love. And in this scale it is knowledge that finally sinks and love that rises."[28] How different this is from the sense of opposition between love and knowledge in Hawthorne's characters. Fearing that knowledge shaped by sexual initiation taints the soul, Dimmesdale and Hilda try to reject both in a frantic effort to scrub at the stain of love.

Maggie, on the other hand, learns from her husband's adultery and determines to manipulate everything and everyone for love. In James knowledge is not antithetical but subservient to love. The importance of knowing is never denied, but the power of love is relentless. Charlotte and the Prince "know" in the senses of sexual transgression and style—what Fanny calls "high intelligence"—but lacking love, their knowledge casts darkness rather than sheds light. Indeed, Charlotte's torment at losing the Prince is compounded by her inability to define the extent of Maggie's awareness. Content with her own brand of knowledge, which for the first half of the novel passes for experience in the ways of the world, Charlotte remains in the dark for most of the second half, firmly shackled to the end of Adam's silken halter, voice quavering in despair. James's irony could not be more exquisite.

As Bayley notes, the triumph of Maggie's knowledge of love over the adulterers' knowledge of transgression is clear in the following exchange when Amerigo misunderstands his wife's accusation that he has had for a long time "*two* relations with Charlotte":

> Something in the tone of it gave it a sense, or an ambiguity, almost
> foolish—leaving Maggie to feel as in a flash how such a consequence,
> a foredoomed infelicity, partaking of the ridiculous even in one of the
> cleverest, might be of the very essence of the penalty of wrong-
> doing. "Oh you may have had fifty—had the same relation with her
> fifty times! It's of the number of *kinds* of relation with her that I
> speak—a number that does n't matter really so long as there was n't
> only the one kind father and I supposed. (2:190–91)

The Prince mistakenly, even naïvely, thinks that Maggie refers to
two specific instances of adultery. She, of course, means his public
relation, blessed by contract, and his private one, stained by transgression: "'Find out for yourself!' she had thrown to Amerigo for her
last word on the question of who else 'knew,' that night of the breaking of the Bowl; and she flattered herself that she had n't since then
helped him, in her clear consistency, by an inch. It was what she had
given him all these weeks to be busy with, and she had again and
again lain awake for the obsession of her sense of his uncertainty
ruthlessly and endlessly playing with his dignity. She had handed
him over to an ignorance" (2:298–99).

Maggie is far from attractive here, and certainly no redeeming angel. Knowledge has momentarily outstripped love. But the Prince
jettisons Charlotte, for reasons involving economics and scandal as
well as romance, and joins his wife in not revealing to his mistress
that the former "knows." One does not forget that from Charlotte's
point of view Maggie is now the thing "hideously behind." A beautiful woman of sexual experience and a passionate exemplar of style,
Charlotte is now isolated by a lack of knowledge when she had
thought to possess all. Unlike Hester, who seizes the opportunity of
knowledge to create, Charlotte can think of nothing except "grop-
ingly" to go on while never knowing. All Maggie permits her at the
end is dignity, but everyone except Charlotte understands that
Maggie deliberately lies to provide her rival with a newfound knowledge which, however false and however ludicrous Charlotte is to accept it, banishes the adulteress to America.

One sympathizes with Charlotte. The expulsion of the desirable
woman signals the absence of beauty. Yet the sterility of her knowledge is finally no match for the creativity of Maggie's imagination.[29]
Aware that the bowl is always cracked, Maggie will now work to
cover it and thereby create the superficial harmony based on knowl-

edge that James insists is necessary for civilized behavior. Her refusal to press for the final extreme of knowledge, to demand that her
husband confess the particulars of the affair, strikes many readers as
inhuman. It is difficult for some to praise a woman whose knowledge
rests partly on not wanting to know. But to label her unreal, at either the height of redemptive angel or the depth of avenging witch,
is to miss the nuance that she acknowledges culpability for isolating
herself and the Prince in different corners of their marriage. The
irony is that Maggie's knowledge is also based on her conscious ignorance, her realization that she should not push the transgressors to
the extremes of scarlet letters and public scandal. One agrees with
Bayley that she compels the adulterers "to be not only good but interesting" by understanding that the protection of their secret is
worth more than the revelation of their duplicity.[30] James shows that
Maggie both knows and refuses to know, and in refusing to know she
rejects the invitation to moral judgment.

What she does know is that she has committed an all too common
error; she has allowed both the financial agreement and the wedding
sacrament to separate her from her husband. Understanding of that
mistake, in itself a kind of transgression, prompts her not to require
the sordid details but to remedy the domestic particulars. Who
loves whom is her most pressing question, and Maggie knows that
she loves the Prince. Another irony in this novel of overlapping
ironies is that she must lie to declare the truth of that love: "If
Charlotte does n't understand me it's because I've prevented her.
I've chosen to deceive her and to lie to her." To the Prince's response
that Charlotte may think her a fool, Maggie replies, "She may think
what she likes" (2:348, 356). Her confidence rests on discovering the reciprocity between love and knowledge, a reciprocity
that Hawthorne's Hilda and several of Updike's women—Janice
Angstrom, Angela Hanema, and Jane Marshfield, for example—shy
away from in bafflement.

Finally, one should not underestimate the power of sex in shaping
Maggie's confidence. Knowledge requires awareness of the snake,
and Maggie is ready for expulsion from the garden. She counters
secret adultery with aggressive passion. James's account of it is not
specific, of course, but the nuance cannot be missed.

Waiting for her husband to return from the weekend with
Charlotte, Maggie realizes that "deep-seated passion" has aches as

well as joys, and that anxiety increases one's consciousness of it.
James does not identify the "force of the feeling" that overwhelms
her, but he leaves little doubt that her need for the Prince is largely
sexual:

> She had never doubted of the force of the feeling that bound her to
> her husband; but to become aware almost suddenly that it had begun
> to vibrate with a violence that had some of the effect of a strain
> would, rightly looked at, after all but show that she was, like thou-
> sands of women, every day, acting up to the full privilege of passion.
> Why in the world should n't she, with every right? (2:7–8)

Unlike Hilda, who represses sexuality, and Hester, who abstains following the initial affair, Maggie now understands that sexual desire
is not at all unusual. Her dilemma is not the moral dimension of sex
but the question of how to regain the "full privilege of passion."
Guilt is not an issue except insofar as she admits the disastrous consequences of her isolation from the Prince. Aware that her "faculties"
have not been "used" for a good while, but confident of her physical
qualities, of her "deep receptacles," Maggie resolves not to expose
her husband but to seduce him. The following passage is among the
most powerful in the book, and with it James looks not backward to
Hawthorne but forward to twentieth-century fiction:

> It had come to the Princess, obscurely at first, but little by little more
> conceivably, that her faculties had n't for a good while been concomi-
> tantly used; the case resembled in a manner that of her once-loved
> dancing, a matter of remembered steps that had grown vague from
> her ceasing to go to balls. She would go to balls again—that seemed,
> freely, even crudely, stated, the remedy; she would take out of the
> deep receptacles in which she had laid them away the various orna-
> ments congruous with the greater occasions and of which her store,
> she liked to think, was none of the smallest. (2:8)

One does not need a Freudian primer to decipher James's metaphor
when Maggie realizes the danger of her situation and glimpses
"across her vision ten times a day the gleam of a bare blade" (2:9).

Placing the repercussions of knowledge, passion, adultery, and
guilt at the heart of *The Golden Bowl*, James breaks with the official
nineteenth-century silence about sexuality in domestic affairs. Many
decades later Updike makes explicit what James makes clear. Sears's
comment is instructive: "James always deals with sexual matters by

some kind of indirection, articulating in disguised form what the Victorians (except for their pornography) generally did not articulate at all."[31] In so doing, he rejects the traditional Victorian ideology that in public—that is, in novels—one does not admit the persuasion of passion. Sex is involved in knowledge; to keep silent about it is to lie. What is radical about James's sophistication is his recognizing that passion within the contract is not the only issue. Sex flourishes beyond the accepted moral boundaries, and people take lovers without the ceremony of love. Maggie must adapt to this truth. Fully conscious of the Prince's "supreme power," she knows that he makes other women long for his masculinity. Love and passion are not necessary companions nor, as James knew, are adults and passion; one need only recall *What Maisie Knew* to realize his understanding of preadolescent interest in sexuality.

Maggie's reaction to the adultery is typically ambiguous in the Jamesian fashion. She yearns to punish the husband who betrays her at the same time that she needs to possess his attentions as a man. She never specifies her desire, but her suggestions are always clear, as in her offer when the Prince returns from the weekend: "How he had looked, for her, during an instant, at the door, before going out, how he had met her asking him, in hesitation first, then quickly in decision, whether she could n't help him by going up with him. He had perhaps also for a moment hesitated, but he had declined her offer, and she was to preserve . . . the memory of the smile with which he had opined that at that rate they would n't dine till ten o'clock" (2:19–20). Listening to her offer, one remembers the forest scene in which Hester lets down her hair.

Sears correctly notes that James's handling of sexual matters offended the official standards of both nineteenth- and twentieth-century readers: the former because he insisted on the universality of sexuality; the latter because he refused to render it directly.[32] One thinks of *The Wings of the Dove* and Kate's agreeing to go alone to Densher's rooms. The Victorian temper protested when James manipulated his young woman in such a crass way, and the modern temper objected when he shut the bedroom door. Yet a point to emphasize is that *The Golden Bowl* is not a metaphorical description of Maggie's longing for the Prince's sexual favors but an account of her growing awareness of her need. To arrive at this knowledge and to win back her husband she must decipher appearances designed to mislead her; to decipher she must admit the power of passion. Determining what is going on—once she allows herself to see—is relatively easy for her. The difficulty is how to take it. Placed for the first time in a false position, she learns that assigning the transgressions to one of the watertight compartments of her moral sense will not do. For Maggie, for James, and for the reader, the challenge is to understand the reverberations of adultery rather than to see the details of the betrayal itself.

James will not point his finger in any one direction. Those who are victimized must share the blame with those who transgress. Insisting on a childlike view of an adult world in which her father is the leading man, Maggie unknowingly cooperates with the Prince and especially with Charlotte, both of whom affirm the flawless harmony of appearances. Although the guilt may not be equal, it is shared. Maggie's self-deception is the other side of Charlotte's selfishness.

Thus in *The Golden Bowl*, the premier novel of adultery in American literature, James begins where nineteenth-century novels of manners traditionally end—with marriage. Aware that the economic contract is more significant than the sacramental ceremony, he links the institution of marriage not to moral directives but to social imperatives. The crack in the bowl is a flaw in society. Both must be covered rather than exposed if civilized behavior is required. But to cover adequately one must first recognize the crack. This Maggie does when she accepts both the relationship between passion and knowledge and the opposition of exposure and harmony. The unattainable goal of supreme happiness is abandoned in favor of a partial avoidance of despair. This lesson reached Updike. More than any other twentieth-century fiction, Updike's marriage novels adapt James's variations on the theme; but unlike his forerunner's characters, Updike's hesitate to give up on happiness.

NOTES

1. Michael Innes, *Money from Holme* (1964; Harmondsworth: Penguin, 1976) 40.

2. Laurence Bedwell Holland calls attention to the echo of Hawthorne in *The Golden Bowl* when he points to the scene in which Maggie hears the

"shriek of a soul in pain" in Charlotte's voice, and compares it to Hester's hearing Dimmesdale's "cry of pain" in the Election Day Sermon. See *The Expense of Vision: Essays on the Craft of Henry James* (Princeton: Princeton University Press, 1964) 333–34.

3. Sallie Sears, *The Negative Imagination: Form and Perspective in the Novels of Henry James* (Ithaca: Cornell University Press, 1968) 161, 162–63.

4. Sears 171.

5. Sears 50.

6. Henry James, "The Art of Fiction," in *The Great Critics: An Anthology of Literary Criticism*, ed. James Henry Smith and Edd Winfield Parks, 3rd ed. (New York: Norton, 1951) 669.

7. John Bayley, *The Characters of Love* (London: Constable, 1960) 214, 217. Bayley continues: James "came to see the deepest and most valuable subject in the side of life which was necessarily and valuably uneventful, the muffled relation in which there was everything to reveal because · nothing was concealed" (247).

8. R. B. J. Wilson, *Henry James's Ultimate Narrative: The Golden Bowl* (St. Lucia, Australia: University of Queensland Press, 1981) 6–7.

9. *The Notebooks of Henry James*, ed. F. O. Matthiessen and Kenneth B. Murdock (1947; New York: Oxford University Press, 1961) 170.

10. *The Notebooks of Henry James* 187–88.

11. *The Letters of Henry James*, 2 vols., ed. Percy Lubbock (New York: Scribner's, 1920) 2:10.

12. *The Notebooks of Henry James* 130.

13. Leon Edel, *Henry James: The Master, 1901–1916* (Philadelphia and New York: Lippincott, 1972) 216, 218. Edel also explains another biographical source for the bowl. James first saw it in 1902 when he learned that George I had presented it to the Lambs, the family that had built the house he owned at the time (209). Bayley offers an interesting comment on the bowl as symbol: "James has often been criticized on the ground that the golden bowl of the story is a rather clumsy and ineffective piece of symbolism, but in fact it is not really a symbol at all, any more than is the handkerchief in *Othello*—both are pieces of dramatic machinery that serve the same function of ritual coincidence" (209).

14. Henry James, "A London Life," *The Complete Tales of Henry James*, 12 vols., ed. Leon Edel (Philadelphia and New York: Lippincott, 1963) 7:88.

15. "A London Life" 93, 94, 97.

16. "A London Life" 105, 135.

17. Edel, introduction, *The Complete Tales*, 7:7, 8.

18. Heath Moon, "James's 'A London Life' and the Campbell Divorce Scandal," *American Literary Realism* 13 (1980):246.

19. Gore Vidal, "Return of 'The Golden Bowl,'" *New York Review of*

Books, 19 Jan. 1984: 8, 9. See "Cracking 'The Golden Bowl,'" *New York Review of Books*, 1 Mar. 1984, for John Bayley's challenge to Vidal's position, and Vidal's reply.

20. Moon 247, 248, 250. See *The Letters of Henry James* 1:124.

21. *The Letters of Henry James* 2:15.

22. *The Letters of Henry James* 2:28, 30. James liked the American edition of *The Golden Bowl*, which he called "charming and readable," but he detested the English edition with its small print and cramped pages and which he described as "fat, vile, small-typed, horrific, prohibitive." See letter (19 Nov. 1905) to H. G. Wells (2:41).

23. *The Letters of Henry James* 2:43. James continued to think well of *The Golden Bowl*, for when Stark Young asked, through Mrs. G. W. Prothero, for guidance in reading James's books, James responded (14 Sept. 1913) with two lists of five titles each. *The Golden Bowl* was included in both lists (*Letters* 2:333).

24. Henry James, *The Golden Bowl*, 2 vols. (New York: Scribner's, 1909) 2:358. Hereafter cited parenthetically.

25. Holland 372.

26. Walter Wright, "Maggie Verver: Neither Saint nor Witch," *Nineteenth Century Fiction* 12 (1957):59–71; Joseph Firebaugh, "The Ververs," *Essays in Criticism* 4 (1954): 406; Sears 210, 212.

27. Dorothea Krook, *The Ordeal of Consciousness in Henry James* (1962; London: Cambridge University Press, 1967) 240.

28. Bayley 218.

29. I cannot agree with Bayley that Charlotte's vitality is based in "the essential resilience of a comedy character" (258) and that her survival at the end indicates a triumph. As marked woman, though not publicly exposed, Charlotte is the banished transgressor expelled from the society that she longs for to the place that she fears. Aware that she despises the United States and wants both the Prince and money, one cannot accept as triumph her exile with money but without the Prince. She does survive, and one is grateful because her anguish touches the reader's sympathy, but one also understands that her survival is largely the result of Maggie's manipulation. Charlotte lands partially on her feet because Maggie will have it so, but her losses are more notable than her gains. Maggie and the reader admire her because she plays her role to the end, yet neither forgets that the truth which she claims for herself—that Maggie hates the marriage between Adam and Charlotte—rests on the firmer foundation of Maggie's lie.

30. Bayley 240.

31. Sears 15 (footnote).

32. Sears 18.

Adultery and Updike's   4
Marriage Novels

enry James offers both a classic tale of illicit love and a portrait of the wife as elusive woman, and the complex combination contributes to the reputation of *The Golden Bowl* as the high point of American novels of adultery. One remembers that Charlotte fails because, among other flaws, she makes transgression too easy for the Prince; and that Maggie wins because, among other strengths, she makes it difficult for the Prince to find out what she knows. Both James and Updike direct the reader's concern to the married couple instead of to the adulterous outcasts, but where James concludes the dilemma with the social harmony reestablished, Updike leaves the matter unresolved. His wayward husbands are always grateful but usually afraid.

One terror is that adultery often results in banishment. From an Eden of passion to an exposure in public is a long fall, as Dimmesdale knows and the Prince fears, and thus the adulterers are always looking for an escape beyond the boundaries of the community. As Tony Tanner notes, "The quest for, or dream of, such an impossible world apart recurs constantly in the novel of adultery—for all available areas of the given world ultimately seem inhospitable to the adulterous lovers."[1] Such a quest, of course, has been a key to Western narrative since the beginning, and Tanner, like Updike, wonders about the future of the novel in a society that no longer cares "much about marriage, and all that is implied in that transaction."[2] Updike, however, would not agree with some of Tanner's prescriptions. Tanner wants the novel of adultery to illustrate "intense passion generated by these classic tales of illicit love." Updike refuses to play that game. Directing sympathy not only to the insecure lovers but also to the despairing married couple, he argues that loss and separation threaten spouses as well as adulterers. In his fiction the wife, not the mistress, is often the woman difficult to win. Maggie learns this lesson in *The Golden Bowl* when she tells the Prince to find out for himself.

Writing in the late twentieth century, Updike must respond to a social milieu different from James's. He is aware of the contrast: "The writer now makes his marks on paper blanker than it has ever been. Our common store of assumptions has dwindled, and with it the stock of viable artistic conventions."[3] *Couples* is the Updike novel that most blatantly illustrates the different set of assumptions, for in its account of adultery sex is what he calls "the emergent religion . . . the only thing left."[4] Like most of Updike's male heroes, Piet Hanema (his name suggests piety and man) suffers the agony of religious doubt and thus turns to the emergent religion to confirm his sense of self. Guilt, he learns, both lacerates and soothes, and he finds himself balanced between an angelic wife who accepts death as part of the natural cycle and who refuses to have more children, and an earthy mistress who is a regular churchgoer and who aborts her pregnancy.

Like James, Updike neither condemns nor embraces sexual betrayal outright. The casual coupling of Lady Castledean and Mr. Blint is clearly an occasion for James's scorn, but he does grant dignity to the Prince's affair with Charlotte. Similarly, Updike satirizes most of the weekend adulteries in *Couples*, but he sympathizes with Piet's desperation to find faith in the emergent religion now that traditional Christianity seems impotent. The difference between the two novelists illustrates different social assumptions. Committed to a traditional societal order, James must end the adultery. Convinced of a loosening of traditional religious ties, Updike watches the church burn in *Couples* and merely moves his new lovers to a new town.

Sex is inadequate to Piet's spiritual needs, but the established balance of contract and ceremony that sustains James's characters no longer applies either. Everything may be terrible in the heart of man, but at least James's people can re-create the bowl by covering up the crack. Such maneuvering is impossible in Updike's fictional world. As he explains, Piet "divorces the supernatural to marry the natural."[5] Unfortunately, the natural may mean mortality. One need only contrast the names of Piet's women—wife Angela and mistress

Foxy—to see him as another American Adam falling from angel to animal. The echoes of Hawthorne's Hilda and Miriam are clear. Like many of Updike's transgressors, Piet views sensual women as eminently desirable and always a threat. Spiritual needs can be overwhelmed by adulterous sex because women like Foxy are linked to the earth and thus to physical sustenance. As Joey Robinson confesses in *Of the Farm*, "My wife is a field." Defined by such earthiness, Updike's women do not usually encourage the kind of spiritual soaring that promises the grace and fluidity for which his male seekers yearn.

Updike's adaptation of his predecessors is even more pointed in *Marry Me: A Romance*. Where James examines social and economic considerations in *The Golden Bowl*, Updike explores individual and spiritual commitments. The former's characters create the gilt that hides the crack, whereas the latter's search for a promise that they will never die. Restoring the balance of contract and ceremony, Maggie resorts to forceful but manipulative action. Hoping for a sign from God that does not come, Jerry Conant imagines three endings for his predicament. Maggie needs passion and knowledge, but Jerry courts passion and guilt. Only by suffering in bed with his mistress does he overcome fear of death with his wife. If he gives up adultery, he faces the stasis of routine and boredom; if he abandons his family, he denies the sacrament of marriage and God. Ruth Conant's struggle to regain her husband recalls Maggie's fight to recover the Prince. For the first time in their lives both women encounter the shadow of a false position. Once again, however, different sets of assumptions inform the contrasts. For one, Ruth is Updike's most sympathetic female character and yet is also an adulteress. For another, the Prince is desirable while Jerry is insecure. His religious faith is childlike while Ruth's ambivalence is mature. Waiting for God to show him the way or for Ruth to make the decisions, he causes suffering that hurts everyone but that makes him feel alive. Like Dimmesdale's, his faith borders on masochism.

I

In "The Future of the Novel," a speech given to the Bristol (England) Literary Society in February 1969, Updike quotes Dr. Johnson on the word *novel*: "a small tale, generally of love."[6] Johnson had in mind the Italian *novelle* as illustrated by Boccaccio, but Updike takes up the suggestion and argues that from Boccaccio through modernism the "pervasive, perhaps obsessive, thread" is love. Acknowledging that such other preoccupations as illness, pain, and making money affect those who live through them, he insists that earning money, for example, is interesting in a novel only if it advances the central character toward "that eventual copulation that seems to be every reader's insatiable and exclusive desire."[7] Since the novel deals primarily with sentiments, it is by nature sentimental: "Erotic love then becomes a symbol, a kind of code for all the nebulous, perishable sensations which we persist in thinking of as *living*." Living and loving are equations for Updike, so much so that he argues with justification that Joyce's Stephen Daedalus is "slightly tedious" because he is not in love: "Not to be in love, the capital N Novel whispers to capital W Western Man, is to be dying."[8]

This tension is significant, for generally fiction depends on an assumption shared by author and reader that society will obstruct sex outside of marriage. Punishment, banishment, or death follows adultery in the traditional novel. But in the contemporary novel adultery is often what Updike calls a "pleasantry," dangerous, perhaps, but hardly fatal. Yet one must not fall into the trap that ensnares some readers and accuse him of undermining the novel by opening the bedroom door. Although a different set of conventions allows him to be more explicit than Hawthorne and James, he too is concerned for the future of fiction if love is no longer the central issue. The "pleasantry" raises an important question: What happens to the novel when long-accepted barriers to love do not impress writers and readers? What happens, asks Updike, if Tristan's sword is blunted: "Remove the genuine prohibitions and difficulty, and the three-dimensional interweave of the Novel collapses, becomes slack and linear."[9]

He has a point. His concern is not that the novel will go the way of the epic but that it will accommodate a shift from love to violence. If hindrances to sexuality are removed, acts of brutality assume center stage. Novels that focus on torture and violence, such novels as Kosinski's *The Painted Bird* and Selby's *Last Exit to Brooklyn*, are a threat to fiction. Updike may exaggerate, yet his position is not that daily brutality should be ignored but that accounts of violence—or adultery—must be "accurately alive to their complicated human context." Gratuitous violence, like gratuitous sex, ignores the humanity that the novel proposes to elucidate. For Updike the human context is all, and the pressing question for the novel is always who loves whom. The following comment, cited earlier, is worth repeating:

> The bourgeois novel is inherently erotic, just as the basic unit of bourgeois order—the family unit built upon the marriage contract—is erotic. Who loves whom? Once this question seems less than urgent, new kinds of novels must be written, or none at all. If domestic stability and personal salvation are at issue, acts of sexual conquest and surrender are important. If the issue is an economic reordering, and social control of the means of production, then sexual attachments are as they are in Mao's China—irrelevant, and the fewer the better.[10]

Two issues are significant here. One is that for Updike individual salvation is as important as domestic stability in novels of love. The other is that the fervor of his warning is part of his acknowledgement of the problem. Rather than bow to criticism that he uses sex gratuitously, he argues the contrary, that his fiction is conservative. His descriptions of who loves whom are more explicit than Hawthorne's or James's, but like his predecessors he considers the obstacles to passion to be the core of the tale.

Updike joins Hawthorne in probing the moral and spiritual repercussions of adultery. His position is clear: "My books are all meant to be moral debates with the reader, and if they seem pointless—I'm speaking hopefully—it's because the reader has not been engaged in the debate. The question is usually, 'What is a good man?' or 'What is goodness?' and in all the books an issue is examined." Confronting his characters with the shadow of cosmic blankness, Updike correctly describes the adulterer Piet Hanema as a moral man who "can't act for himself because he's overwhelmed by the moral implications of any act—leaving his wife, staying with her."[11] A similar dilemma is explored in *Marry Me*, one that illustrates Updike's variation on James's novel of domestic breakdown. Not fear of social exposure but terror of moral damnation causes the aura of desperation in his fiction. Beds may be visited and spouses swapped, but the weight of guilt hangs heavy.

The Novels

The result, of course, is pain: "The general social contract—living with other people, driving cars on highways—all this is difficult, it's painful. It's a kind of agony really—the agony vents itself in ulcers internally, rage externally. . . . In short, all of our institutions—of marriage, the family, your driver's license—everything is kind of precarious, and maintained at a cost of tension."[12] Convinced that much of the tension begins in the bedroom, Updike does not consider his work as part of the contemporary effort to exhaust eroticism by overexposing the subject and debasing the act. His concern is always with the human context, never the clinch itself. Note the implication that the difference between his novels and those of the nineteenth century is more a matter of detail than of focus:

> If you're going to have sex in a book, you really ought to have it. You should go into it enough to try to show what happens, to make it a human transaction. The convention of closing the bedroom's doors that worked so well for the Victorians doesn't seem honest applied to today's world. Yet, despite the freedom the contemporary writer enjoys, in a way we are comparatively bloodless. Certainly, the reader has no doubt that Tolstoy's people are sexually alive: every page is full of an animal solidity. All those novels seem to me to float on the assumption that sex is just enormously interesting.[13]

Hawthorne and James respond to the same interest. The difference is that Updike, in his words, brings "coitus out of the closet and off the altar" and puts it "on the continuum of human behavior." Admitting that sexual events are "huge but not all-eclipsing," he urges novelists to "give them their size."[14] This he does by taking a cue from chivalric romances and Denis de Rougemont. The question in his marriage novels is whether passion can survive marriage. In James the dilemma is often the threat that illicit sex poses to both moral value and social order, but in Updike the conflict is not between individual morality and social style—what James's Fanny Assingham calls "high intelligence"—but between marriage itself and passion. Marriage may have the sanction of ceremony, but adultery promises the freedom of desire. This is why Ruth Conant's comment is ironic: "Any romance that does not end in marriage fails."[15] If, as is often the case in Updike's fiction, the adulterer is also a believer, then his crisis is not fear of exposure as it is in Hawthorne and James but fear for his soul. Yet paradoxically the pursuit of passion is also the denial of death. One seeks life in a lover.

Still, the integrity of the social contract remains an issue. Harmony is not as central to Updike as it is to James, but he acknowledges that the dash to freedom leaves havoc behind. His contrast of Don Juan and Tristan is revealing: "Don Juan loves Woman under the guise of many women, exhaustingly. . . . for which Society does not thank him, because its effects are all disruptive. Whereas to love Woman under the guise of one woman who repeatedly escapes leaves the social fabric intact, conserves physical energy, and induces a possibly creative private pain."[16] Hester, Miriam, and Maggie all respond creatively to a similar pain induced by passion, and with their examples as a frame Updike tries to remedy what he calls the "notoriously thin" portraits of women in American fiction: "We may have reached that point of civilization, or decadence, where we *can* look at women."[17]

Updike's males do indeed look, and they do so from a point of view that often combines Tristan and Don Juan. Reacting to traditional Western efforts to elevate the former over the latter, Updike points out that while society may thus be maintained and art created, love is more than a command to procreate the race and to provide acceptable limits for commerce between the sexes. A fundamental anxiety in his marriage novels is not destruction of the race or dismantling of the social harmony but recognition that the individual will die. Love and even adultery offer value in the cave of existential despair: "Only in being loved do we find external corroboration of the supremely high valuation each ego secretly assigns itself."[18] Choosing a lover outside the ceremony is more than insisting on the freedom to choose; it is selecting a partner who through sexual consummation validates the existence of the self. Against the claims of the anxiety to confirm one's life in the face of annihilation by death, the counterclaims of extending the race and protecting social propriety seem petty. The following opinion is crucial to a proper understanding of Updike's fiction: "The heart *prefers* to move against the grain of circumstance; perversity is the soul's very life. Therefore the enforced and approved bonds of marriage, restricting freedom, weaken love."[19]

The Prince would appreciate this sentiment, as indeed would

Hawthorne and James, because each understands the negative equation between sexual intensity and social approval. Marriage is enforced by the ceremonial code and notarized by the contractual law, but confirmation of one's existence requires passion, and passion demands freedom. The difference is that love in marriage is a paradox for Updike; it promises physical life to the race and spiritual death to the progenitors. For all his inability to express himself, Rabbit Angstrom senses this truth:

> He feels the truth: the thing that has left his life has left irrevocably; no search would recover it. No flight would reach it. It was here, beneath the town, in these smells and these voices, forever behind him. The fullness ends when we give Nature her ransom, when we make children for her. Then she is through with us, and we become, first inside, and then outside, junk.[20]

Marriage is shaky but adultery promising when Updike's characters acknowledge Rabbit's dilemma. *Too Far to Go* is an example. The story of a long decision to say good-bye, this unified collection of tales traces the decline of commitment through transgression and toward divorce. The possibility of public scandal that Dimmesdale and the Prince fear never occurs to Updike's couple. Nothing hasty and very little of the dramatic occurs in *Too Far to Go*; indeed, husband and wife resist the final parting. But when it comes, Updike ironically shows that their no-fault divorce case resembles their wedding ceremony many years ago when they were both young and lovely and when passion was bright and new. One definition of marriage in *Too Far to Go* is "a million mundane moments shared." Updike's foreword insists that all things, including marriage, terminate: "That a marriage ends is less than ideal; but all things end under heaven, and if temporality is held to be invalidating, then nothing real succeeds. The moral of these stories is that all blessings are mixed."[21] What a variation this is on the moral stance in more traditional American domestic fiction.

II

Updike's marriage novels usually focus on a male narrator who suffers the tension generated by the conflict between the illusions that caress him from the past and the demands that lacerate him in the present. Love and hope nourished in his youth become memory and desire pounding in his maturity. Where have all the flowers gone? is not an empty question to the Updike narrator who moves toward the ashes on the other side of middle age. The liberation that he struggles to receive from his parents becomes the trap that he works to escape from with his wife. The happiness that he glimpses in "Flight" is the pain that he suffers in "Separating." As the narrator explains in "The Music School," "we are all pilgrims, faltering toward divorce."

As marriage is impossible for Hester and Dimmesdale, so divorce is unthinkable for Maggie and the Prince. Yet James's concern for the necessity of social harmony is unfeasible in Updike's world of individual angst. Where the former's characters hope to step beyond the present toward the future, the latter's long to duck behind the present toward the past. Rabbit has more in mind than basketball when he thinks, "They've not forgotten him: worse, they never heard of him." Looking at his granddaughter in *Rabbit Is Rich*, he sees another nail in his coffin. No wonder he turns to the past and asks what happened to the social imperative to fly. The teen-age flight degenerates to the adult run, and the male narrator resorts to adultery and divorce for signs that he still lives. "Preach! Write! Act! Do anything, save to lie down and die!" pleads Hester to her lover. Sensing death in the insistence of the daily routine, Updike's transgressors take her at her word.

Where economic considerations affect adultery in *The Golden Bowl*, and where notions of sin defeat love in *The Scarlet Letter*, individual integrity leads to adultery in *Couples* and *Marry Me*. This is one of the central ironies of the Updike canon. Promising to love and cherish his wife, the Updike male learns that he does so at risk to the self. Thus while marriage is more ceremony than contract in Updike, it encourages the religious pitfall of despair. Caught between the religiously blessed ceremony and the religiously defined sin, the transgressor reaches out toward adultery in an effort to rekindle the liveliness he has lost. The sexual desire of Amerigo merges with the religious sensibility of Dimmesdale, and the Updike novel of adultery reflects the late twentieth century, when individual need counts for more than social stability. As Jane Barnes remarks in one of the key essays on Updike, the narrator's duty is not business but awareness: "His first responsibility is to know the *meaning* of life; what he should do, how he should live."[22]

The only way to live is not to die. When Jerry Conant decides that he is married to his death, he runs to Sally for adultery on the beach beside the immortal ocean. The mystery that he pursues in the womb of women defines his relationship with wife and mistress. In both cases the moral restrictions on sex inhibit the moral imperative to know, and the reciprocity between sexuality and knowledge that Hawthorne and James develop becomes a quagmire of confusion for the Updike male who fears death. Security guaranteed by his mother in the past and challenged by his wife in the present becomes, he hopes, immortality promised by his mistress in the future. The irony is that if he stays with the wife he dies; if he runs to the mistress he sins. The responsibilities of the wedding ceremony diminish the potentialities for freedom, and the Updike adulterer is trapped between virtue and wishing, duty and desire.

Constantly on the lookout for love, he forever tries to create a new life. Dimmesdale cannot act, and the Prince waits for Maggie to act for him, but Rabbit and Piet and Jerry hope to force the new Eden if only by moving to the next bedroom or the next suburb. Love is always the key to the re-creation of the self, but love often conflicts with sacrament. If he loves the mistress, yet cannot leave the wife, he turns the imperative to act into the trap of stasis. Understanding James's account of adultery, but unwilling to bow to a nineteenth-century public norm, Updike unites both James and Hawthorne in applying a religious sensibility to a social dilemma. If his adulterer remains with the wife, he hurts both himself and her; if he transgresses with the mistress, he also hurts both, but at least he creates a new promise of happiness. A Hawthornian sense of sin conflicts with a Jamesian definition of love, and the Updike adulterer often finds himself stymied when he knows that he ought to run. Transgression means both joy and guilt; fidelity means both absolution and death. Updike's males have no Maggie Verver to work the magic of sexual excitement and domestic harmony. If they will have the former, they must follow Hester Prynne beyond the confines of the community to the freedom of the forest. Vitality is defined as immorality, and the Hawthornian stain seeps through.

Where Hawthorne forces Hester to cover her breasts and hide her hair, James shows Maggie unpacking her gowns to "go to balls again." In both cases the sexual implications are clear. The moral nature that James attributes to Hawthorne becomes a social nature in *The Golden Bowl*. Updike accepts James's mandate for sexuality but frames it in Hawthorne's concept of guilt. Insisting that sexual happiness does matter, the adulterer wonders whether the marriage ceremony dims the glow; understanding that adultery is sin, he worries for the immortality of his soul. Sex sits at the center of both dilemmas. The desires of the individual clash with the demands of society, and Updike's fiction locates itself between Hawthorne and James. Social order is stronger than the individual for both of the earlier authors, but in *The Golden Bowl* James accommodates duty and desire in a superficial yet necessary balance that Hawthorne cannot consider. Updike turns from Hawthorne's repression of sex, but he cannot embrace James's acceptance of society.

Updike understands, of course, that in characterizing his adulterer to want both morality and transgression, wife and mistress, he makes the male appear weak. In taking two steps toward divorce and one step back toward marriage, the transgressor exhausts his family, himself, and the reader. The greater availability of sexual choice that Updike posits as a given in the late twentieth century results not in increased freedom but in magnified indecision. Such existential irony does not plague the adulterers of Hawthorne and James.[23] Realizing that transgression is action, but fearing for the stainlessness of his soul, Updike's adulterer finds himself vacillating even as he moves to act. The result is that the reader loses patience with Piet and Jerry although he sympathizes with their predicaments. It is as if the unimaginative, all-but-sexless wife, the personification of social duty, deserves better than the frantic, sexually promiscuous husband. Janice Angstrom may be dull, cloying, and middle-aged at only twenty-six, but one understands her frustration at Rabbit's waffling between Ruth and home. Rabbit's running leads him to a standstill—no wonder Ruth calls him Mr. Death. Yet he is one of the most earnest of Updike's transgressors, and for the best of them the search for sexual happiness is also a moral quest for God. Were it not for this sense of religious dread, the reader might entirely lose sympathy with the wayward husband. Take away the spiritual yearning

108

The Novels

and the adulterer seems juvenile. But when he repudiates selfishness, when he realizes that commitment to the mistress engages
the specter of death as quickly as fidelity to the wife, then he understands that his erotic frustrations are emblematic of the spiritually
unfulfilled life. To be totally satisfied is also to be dead. Sexual longing is painful, but pain is a sign that he lives.

Watching Updike's philanderer flay himself with alternating bouts
of transgression and guilt, one encounters Dimmesdale in suburbia.
The minister's self-laceration, his voyeurism of the soul, is more terrible than any punishment of Updike's lovers, but this is partly because he has no place to run. Hester's successful transfer of erotic
energy into art permits her to escape the guilt that the iron men and
their opinions would have her suffer. Afraid of Hester's creative
skills, Dimmesdale must flog his soul to ease his conscience. Yet pain
is life, the surest sign of his lingering humanity. Once he confesses
his guilt, he dies. More consciously than any other late-twentieth-
century American novelist, Updike adapts Hawthorne's probing of
the relationships among sex, guilt, and belief. A primary difference
is that his adulterer accepts the lesson that Hawthorne's rejects: that
guilt can boost life as well as drag it down. Two examples come to
mind, one from the novel *Rabbit, Run* and the other from the short
story "Domestic Life in America." In the former, Rabbit responds to
a minister's attempt to make him conform by hitting a perfect tee
shot that illustrates the grace, the fluidity, the sheer flight that
he seeks:

> The sound has a hollowness, a singleness he hasn't heard before. His
> arms force his head up and his ball is hung way out. . . . It recedes
> along a line straight as a ruler-edge. Stricken; sphere, star, speck. It
> hesitates, and Rabbit thinks it will die, but he's fooled, for the ball
> makes his hesitation the ground of a final leap: with a kind of visible
> sob takes a last bite of space before vanishing in falling, "That's *it!*" he
> cries and, turning to Eccles with a smile of aggrandizement, repeats,
> "That's it."[24]

In the latter example the restless husband equates the guilt of unsanctioned sexual pleasure with the erotic intensity of swimming:
"It was as when, tired and dirty from work, Fraser had stripped and
given himself to that sustaining element, the water in the center of

the channel, which answered every movement of his with a silken resistance and buoyed him above its own black depth." [25]

In both cases the sensation of soaring, of being buoyed beyond the void of the bottomless depth, comes from adultery framed by guilt and belief. The irony is that the flight is ephemeral. Immoral adultery may finally damn the soul, but moral fidelity will eventually cramp the spirit. To indulge the former is to follow Hawthorne into the forest; to accept the latter is to join James in the drawing room. In neither instance, suggests Updike, is harmony possible. Most of his women lack Maggie's sexual awakening and her discovery of the necessary ratio of manners to passion. Not how to preserve the superficial order but how to save the self is finally the problem. What a diminishment this is from Hawthorne's understanding of the complexity of sin and from James's knowledge of the terrible in the heart of man. The reduction of the individual in the face of the enormous pressures of the twentieth century has likewise reduced the turmoil of adultery to a personal level. Social dissolution is always a possibility, but the Updike transgressor worries mostly about himself.

III

The religious sensibility standing behind Updike's adulterers is not only the rigorous Puritanism of Hawthorne but also the conservative theology of Kierkegaard and Karl Barth. Father George W. Hunt has provided the most cogent general account of their impact on Updike, and in the first chapter of his study he explains for the lay person how Kierkegaard and Barth resisted all efforts to liberalize Christianity. [26] Not blasphemy but humanism was the enemy, and the result was that both theologians rejected the modern tendency to domesticate God by interpreting God's tenets in terms of bourgeois ethics. This is what the Reverend Tom Marshfield has in mind when he criticizes his wife's liberalism in A Month of Sundays. She is a good person but a slack believer, ethical and soft where Marshfield is Barthian and hard. Such a staunchly conservative theology elevates belief over ethics, revelation over rationalism, as the dour Reverend Kruppenbach preaches to the liberal Reverend Eccles in Rabbit, Run:

I know what they teach you at seminary now: this psychology and
that. But I don't agree with it. You think now your job is to be an un-
paid doctor, to run around and plug up the holes and make everything smooth. I don't think that. . . . If Gott wants to end misery
He'll declare the Kingdom now. . . . I say you don't know what your
role is or you'd be home locked in prayer. *There* is your role: to make
yourself an exemplar of faith. . . . There is nothing but Christ for us.
All the rest, all this decency and busyness, is nothing. It is Devil's
work. [27]

As Hunt notes, Kierkegaard and Barth "stressed the radical cen-
trality of Revelation and the importance of reasserting the 'orthodox'
beliefs of Christianity articulated in the early creeds and stressed by
the early Protestant Reformers such as Luther and Calvin." [28] The
Kierkegaard-Barth orthodoxy is complicated theological business,
but an acceptable oversimplification for the reader of Updike is that
unquestioning belief is more important than good works. If, as
Barth argues, man cannot reach God but only God can touch man,
then man's duty is rigorously to follow the first stipulation of the
Apostles' Creed: I believe in God the Father. Armed with belief,
confident that grace in all its manifestations can be earned, Updike's
male adulterers cause pain but hope to avoid damnation. Unlike
Dimmesdale, they are not always rendered immobile by the conflict
between erotic demands and spiritual needs. Although they grieve
for the hurt they bring their families, they nevertheless continue to
pursue the unity of flesh and spirit that Puritanism ripped asunder.
Marshfield is as conservative in his theology as Dimmesdale, but
unlike his predecessor he believes not only in God but also in the
spiritual worth of the flesh. Hawthorne's threat of damnation and
James's warning of social dissolution become in Updike the terror of
individual angst. No wonder Rabbit Angstrom dashes uphill from his
daughter's funeral while the other mourners wallow below in hu-
manistic sympathy. The only one to believe that his dead baby is in
heaven, he runs from the "right" way toward the "good" way.
Updike's point is that the good way is defined not by social expecta-
tion but by personal belief. Sensing that all truth, including moral
imperatives and religious faith, is never absolute, Rabbit must continue his run if he is to continue his life. The transgression of his
adultery is finally not the paramount issue. As Updike explains,

"Everything unambiguously expressed seems somehow crass to me. . . . I feel that to be a person is to be in a situation of tension, is to be in a dialectical situation. A truly adjusted person is not a person at all."[29]

The ambiguity of moral imperatives in Updike's fiction frustrates many readers, but this expression of Kierkegaardian relativity propels his characters toward the resoluteness of faith. Marshfield and Rabbit can live with the relative; Dimmesdale cannot—and therein lies a key difference between Updike's world and Hawthorne's. In this sense Updike reflects James's refusal to evaluate violation of contract in terms of right and wrong. The moral debate may move toward an understanding of the good, but the definition is never definite. Recall Updike's comment: "My books are meant to be moral debates with the reader. . . . The question is usually, 'What is a good man?' or 'What is goodness?'" His insistence on the relativity of good and evil likely has its genesis in Barth's explanation that evil can have only a relative existence because it is not part of God's positive plan for creation.[30] Hunt's metaphor is instructive: evil is the shadow to God's light; without the latter the former cannot exist. Although such commentators as John Gardner may complain when they forward the claims of a simplistic moral fiction, Updike joins James in generally refusing to create thoroughly good or evil characters. He combines Hawthorne's religious sensibility and James's social concerns to write a fiction of adultery in which the black and white of moral judgments are rendered an ambiguous gray.

Hawthorne's grasp of the unity of Jonathan Edwards's Puritan heritage and Emerson's Transcendental idealism frames the decisions that many of his characters must make. James's and Updike's characters suffer similar dilemmas: if transgression is a sign of man's imperfection and thus his entry to the world from the garden, how does he reconcile the command to be human with the commandment to go and sin no more? James may develop Maggie's flaws in terms of social impropriety rather than spiritual stain, but her problem recalls those of Hilda and Dimmesdale, Miriam and Hester, Rabbit and Jerry Conant. Although Updike has a greater sense of nostalgia for the lost innocence of the garden, he joins his two predecessors in appreciating the paradox generated by the conflicting demands to avoid the stain and to live in the world. To insist on one or the other is to fall to the fallacy of moral absoluteness; to combine the two is to accept the paradoxically firmer ground of ambiguity.

Those desiring an analysis of Kierkegaard's association of sex with guilt, sin, and dread may consult Father Hunt's book. I am more interested in Updike's general use of adultery than in his specific borrowings from Kierkegaardian theology, but it is relevant to underscore Hunt's paraphrase of Kierkegaard's differentiation between sin and guilt. In Kierkegaardian terms sin is a "specification of guilt, a clarification of it," while guilt is a universal sense of unease that touches all humanity. Sin is often finite, guilt infinite in its ramifications, and thus the latter is much more encompassing than mere unhappiness, much more a spiritual quality. As a result, writes Hunt, "no outsider can appreciate another's guilt, for he will erroneously transpose it into quantitative terms; being a spiritual condition, guilt is always a private affair."[31]

Updike is quite serious in his assertion of the necessity for personal faith. Noting that today most American Protestants play at being disciples of Calvin or Luther and thus have difficulty conceiving of both a judging God and a diabolical devil, he wonders if Americans can "morally tolerate the God who would permit such an opponent to arise, who would arm him with death and pain, who would allow suffering Mankind to become one huge Job, teased and tested in heavenly play."[32] The result of this slip from rigorous faith is that Americans resist the pain of Judgment Day and "grant" God his existence by a leap of faith, "incidentally reducing his 'ancient foe' to the dimensions of a bad comic strip."[33] Describing himself as a "feeble believer," and insisting that belief in God automatically imposes on the universe a structure that requires such support systems as a devil, Updike refers his reader to Barth's *Church Dogmatics* for a systematic definition of evil as "nothingness," as, in Barth's words, "that which God does not will. . . . For not only what God wills, but what He does not will, is potent, and must have a real correspondence."

No comic strip devil here; Updike clearly believes with Barth—and with Dimmesdale—in the reality of evil: "A potent 'nothingness' was unavoidably conjured up by God's creating *something*. The existence of something demands the existence of *something else*."[34] Although they are never theologians and rarely thinkers (except for

Marshfield), Updike's transgressors fear the void of Barth's nothingness. They long for grace even while they pursue their neighbors' wives. Updike borrows from Barth the tenet of faith that argues that man's tendency to stray, his placement in a dialectical situation, determines his humanness: "A creature freed from the possibility of falling away would not really be living as a creature." Only God is perfect; man is defined by his freedom to fall away, to sin, to transgress. Thus, asks Updike, "What man can exempt, from his purest sexual passion and most chivalrous love, the itch to defile?" The natural human condition is to rebel against the order, to insist on individuality by a contrary act; for, writes Updike, "our precious creaturely freedom . . . finds self-assertion in defiance and existence in sin."[35]

This is the freedom that Rabbit runs toward and Jerry Conant pursues when each abandons wife for mistress. Updike argues that "Barth's formulas fit": humanity must resist what is good for it if it hopes to remain human. Yet Barth's other prescription also fits, his insistence that unwavering faith is the antidote to the lure of nothingness. Admitting that he is a Christian because he willingly professes the Apostles' Creed, Updike touches on the Barthian paradox that shapes many of his characters: their belief in Christianity and their eagerness to violate its laws. As he writes in "Faith in Search of Understanding," once again echoing Barth, "The real God, the God men do not invent, is *totaliter aliter*—Wholly Other. We cannot reach Him; only He can reach us. This He has done as the Christ of Biblical revelation."[36] That Rabbit commits adultery with Ruth in an apartment across the street from a church is no accident. Even while he transgresses, Rabbit can honestly tell Ruth that he believes. If the church were removed from Updike's marriage novels, guilt would hardly be an issue.

The expulsion from the garden that Hawthorne explores in *The Marble Faun*, James in *The Golden Bowl*, and Updike in *Couples* and *Marry Me* awakens the sleeping innocents to the power of choice and plunges them into the dilemma of body versus soul. Sex is thus clearly a primary consideration, and guilt shackles those who dare to choose. But where Hawthorne struggles to make Hilda avoid the choice even while he fills the novel with the symbolism of sexuality, James and Updike, at least in *The Golden Bowl* and *Marry*

Me, understand the necessity of sexual commitment. Maggie's renewed ardor is more socially than spiritually directed, while many of Updike's heroes hope to reunify the body and soul that the Puritans split, but in both cases the sexual imperative is acknowledged. The difference is that for Updike erotic experience is morally ambiguous. Rabbit and Jerry try to combat the shrinking of their spirits within marriage by pursuing the mystery of Other in the guise of women. Like Hester and Maggie, they turn transgression into an opportunity for creativity.

Because eroticism—even adultery—unifies the physical and the spiritual, the transgression may be both ethically wrong and spiritually right. The ambiguity of adultery is the key. Piet Hanema is a variation in Updike because in choosing Foxy over Angela he abandons pursuit of the soul for surety of the body. Updike's other characters are not so ready to concede defeat. They understand that in sex they both brush immortality and prefigure death, for the intensity of the encounter is short-lived. This paradox does not interest Hawthorne and James, but Updike suggests that in fleeing the death of eroticism in marriage his characters rush toward mortality in the lure of adultery. Although moralistic notions of good and evil do not obtain, guilt is ever present.

IV

In *Couples*, a thorough dissection of suburban sex, Updike exchanges Hawthorne's and James's metaphors for explicitness. Yet despite the near clinical documentation of sexuality *Couples* is, insists Updike, more about sex as religion. The interests of James and Hawthorne meet in this novel, which places adultery at the center of social harmony and religious nuance. Although many of the casual couplings are ridiculed, Piet's adultery is seriously cast in the mold of spiritual quest. If twentieth-century life denies the opportunities for romance and salvation that are offered to Tristan and Bunyan's Pilgrim, then sex may indeed be the only thing left, the only way that a person can unify conflicting demands. Updike's pilgrims are adulterers, but they hope to escape death and find immortality at the same time. Blake's watercolor of a sleeping Adam and Eve that adorns the dust jacket of *Couples* is ultimately an ironic comment on Piet's final banishment to another suburb from the fallen world of the "post-pill paradise." *Couples* depicts, then, society after Maggie has accepted the burden of knowledge and Hester has put on the A.

Faced with a vague yearning for the security of faith, and armed with the protection of the omnipresent pill, the adulterers in *Couples* have combined to form a new congregation in Hawthorne's Massachusetts for whom the church steeple with its obviously erotic weathercock symbolizes the unity of religion and sex. As the narrator explains, "Children in the town grew up with the sense that the bird was God."[37] Hawthorne consigns his adulterers to the scaffold, while James sends his back to America, but Updike finds his in church. Living in the shadows of the fallen Dimmesdale and Adam Verver is Piet, a man who longs for the prelapsarian stainlessness of his parents' greenhouse. But just as Dimmesdale enters the forest and Adam Verver rifles the Golden Isles, so Piet has been expelled from the sanctuary of the hothouse to the bedrock of society. One may profitably see Adam, Tristan, or even Don Juan in Piet, but the stately ghosts of Hawthorne and James also stand behind him.

Like the dichotomies of Hester in the forest and Hester in the town, of Miriam and Hilda, and of Charlotte and Maggie, the opposition of Piet's two women is a paradigm for the choice that he must make. A lover of stars, Angela seems otherworldly in her ethereal beauty. Foxy is clearly the foil, a desirable woman with an animal appetite. But as Updike adapts the sensibilities of his predecessors in *Couples* and investigates transgression in his own time, he conspicuously denies to Piet the creativity often emanating from adultery that Hawthorne and James take pains to stress. No beautiful A or little Pearl or mended bowl for Piet. Not only do Foxy and Piet indulge in oral sex but they abort the one sign of creation begun by their more conventional coupling. Piet may quest for spiritual surety in adultery, but the fruit of his labor is sterility. It is as if he abandons the promise of creativity when he leaves the heavenly Angela. Updike is conscious of the allusions to sterility in *Couples*. Commenting on the frequency of oral sex in the novel, he notes, "It's a way of eating, eating the apple, of knowing. . . . in De Rougemont's book on Tristram and Iseult he speaks of the sterility of the lovers and Piet and Foxy are sterile vis-a-vis each other."[38]

Similarly, Piet is aware that his adultery is his fall: "My whole life

seems just a long falling" (312). Many of his statements sound pomp-
ous when read out of context, but the modernity of his crisis is clear.
Suffering guilt in his life and dread in his soul, he is an updated
Dimmesdale who rejects the temptation to scourge the body in order to purge the spirit. Rather than peer inward as a voyeur of the
self, he turns outward as an adulterer who still believes. His sense of
quest is obvious when he explains to Foxy that adultery is "a way of
giving yourself adventures. Of getting out in the world and seeking
knowledge" (343). Foxy does not share his fear of mocking God because she accepts his statement that God is between her legs. Yet
when he learns that she is pregnant, his terror takes on Dimmesdale's Calvinistic burden, and he prays to a vindictive God that the
pregnancy be aborted and that Foxy take the blame: "He had been
innocent. . . . She had demanded that he know" (376). Unfortunately for Piet, only Angela is a "messenger of this God," and he has
deserted her. Expelled from the greenhouse, he must turn to the
impotent Freddy Thorne, court jester and lord of misrule for the
couples, to perform the abortion that will signal his fall to sterility.
Freddy's definition of redemption parodies Dimmesdale's prideful
Election Day Sermon: "In the western world there are only two
comical things: the Christian Church and naked women. . . . Everything else tells us we're dead" (146). One recalls Dimmesdale's pon-
tificating about a "glorious destiny for the newly gathered people of
the Lord" while Hester lingers nearby with the scarlet A burning on
her breast. As Dimmesdale is literally banished from the world
when he dies, so Piet must leave the security of the post-pill paradise. His exit with Foxy is marked by an apocalyptic sign of the Calvinist God's displeasure: the church with the wondrous steeple
burns. Yet ironically the cock is saved, the superficial order is re-
stored, and the sterile couples huddle in their fallen world together.

   With its Jamesian emphasis on social detail and its Hawthornian
allusions to adultery, guilt, and belief, *Couples* reflects the sensibilities of both of Updike's predecessors. In *Marry Me*, however,
the backward glance is primarily toward Hawthorne. The epigraph
from Robert Herrick and the subtitle "A Romance" lead the way:
Updike pointedly directs the reader from the formal properties of
the Jamesian novel to the fantasy realm of the Hawthornian tale.
Setting *Marry Me* in the Camelot era of President Kennedy is a

clue, but Updike clarifies the connection even more: "It's my last romance—about romantic love. A romance operates on a slightly different principle from a novel. Instead of muscles it has springs and trap doors. It's something of a valentine. It's meant to have the texture of the fabulous."[39] Updike's valentine embraces the fabulous when it isolates the characters in a less than fantastic but more than mundane setting. Reminiscent of *The Scarlet Letter* with Hester and Dimmesdale as the only lovers in the Puritan community, *Marry Me* focuses on the reveries and repercussions of adultery between two couples in the lost fairy tale of the early 1960s. Their town is appropriately named Greenwood.

Sally defines the dilemma that Jerry refuses to accept: "If you can't take me as a wife, don't spoil me as a mistress" (52). But Jerry cannot act. Marriage to Ruth means the death of his freedom, but adultery with Sally means a stain on his soul. Thus it is interesting that he couches his reply in terms of the international theme that Hawthorne began and James made famous: "But I don't *want* you as a mistress; our lives just aren't built for it. Mistresses are for European novels. Here, there's no institution except marriage" (53). What he really seeks is a wife-mistress, but both the circumstances of culture and the prescriptions of morality do not permit it. The primary obstruction for Jerry is the residue of guilt. Guilt and its twin, fear, are the modern equivalents of Tristan's sword. Jerry fears eternal damnation because he knows that while the shaky moral code promises freedom, it still promotes guilt. He feels trapped by the old morality that is strong enough to torment him but weak enough to let him wander.

A frustrated artist (he designs television commercials), Jerry understands the implications of living in a town named Greenwood. He searches for "clean-swept Nature" on the beach when he commits adultery with Sally; he alludes to Tristan when he speaks of an ideal love that will die if it is ever realized; and he sees himself as a new Adam when he describes the two of them as "the original man and woman." Yearning for the idyll of Romance in the realism of the world, he wants Hawthorne's forest without Chillingworth, but he is always afraid. The wine that he and Sally drink following transgression parodies Communion—the bottle is broken and Jerry cuts his nose. One hears the echo of the ancient response: "This is my blood." James changed the novel of manners by beginning where it traditionally ends, with marriage; Updike goes a step further by beginning with adultery. But while both authors develop the sexual and experiential obligations of knowledge, Updike discusses the spiritual nuance as well. Jerry's idyll with Sally which opens *Marry Me* is punctured by the cut nose and the guilty refrain "*I know. I know.*" No wonder the other characters question his innocence when they know that suffering is the lot of mankind.

With an understanding of Hawthorne's term Romance that detractors of *Marry Me* ignore, Updike appreciates the crises of Dimmesdale and Hilda that place them in the quandary of desiring the apple but fearing the bite. Jerry is as unattractive as they often are, but one offers sympathy because of the genuineness of their suffering. The difference, of course, is that childish Jerry is no agonizing Dimmesdale. Updike makes quite clear that the anguish of Hawthorne's world is not possible in the post-pill paradise. Yet Jerry nevertheless worries about the opposition of sexual transgression and spiritual longing. While his friends accept the unplanned unfolding of events, he believes in "choices, in mistakes, in damnation, in the avoidance of suffering" (45). He wants the pleasures of adultery without the knowledge that everything is terrible in the heart of man.

The terror of knowledge and the fear of damnation make him like a child with too much candy and not enough time to choose. Death is his ultimate blankness, for guilt persuades him that adultery shrinks the soul. Thus when his wife responds to his shock of mortality by mumbling in her sleep "dust to dust," he is terrified and outraged. He lives the paradox that freezes Updike's twentieth-century believer: the freedom from death that he finds with the mistress promises a loss of immortality for betraying the wife. As Jerry tells Ruth, "Whenever I'm with her . . . I know I'm never going to die. . . . You're death. . . . I'm married to my death" (144). His suspicion of her more practical faith is explicit: "She was a Unitarian, and what did this mean, except that her soul was one unit removed from not being there at all?" (96). Jerry craves far more than one unit of protection. He belongs in Hawthorne's century, when smiling Transcendentalism contended with gloomy Calvinism for the future of man's spirit. His expression of Updike's paradox of the twilight of the old morality all but defines him: Dimmesdale might have said the same thing.

The conclusion of *Marry Me* is a conscious echo of the ending of *The Marble Faun*. Recall Hawthorne's postscript and his explanation of being frustrated by repeated requests from literal-minded readers for clarification of his Romance: "There comes to the Author, from many readers of the foregoing pages, a demand for further elucidations respecting the mysteries of the story." "Reluctantly" availing himself of the opportunity, Hawthorne reminds the reader of the difference between Romance and novel before he ironically fills in some details: "The necessity makes him sensible that he can have succeeded but imperfectly, at best, in throwing about this Romance the kind of atmosphere essential to the effect at which he aimed. He designed the story and the characters to bear, of course, a certain relation to human nature and human life, but still to be so artfully and airily removed from our mundane sphere, that some laws and proprieties of their own should be implicitly and insensibly acknowledged."[40] Offering his readers the freedom of an inconclusive conclusion, he finds that they are insecure without more than "a certain relation" to reality.

Updike does not offer an ironic postscript, but he does follow Hawthorne's lead in *The Marble Faun* and includes multiple conclusions to *Marry Me*. In one Jerry and the mistress disembark from a plane in Wyoming: adultery wins. In another Jerry and the wife descend at Nice: adultery loses. In a third Jerry gets off alone at St. Croix: decisions are avoided. Although he argues that Satan is finally routed and Christ revenged, he still seems frozen in Updike's paradox. Safe in the realm of Hawthornian Romance, he will not have to decide between wife and mistress in the world of Jamesian realism. Either preference, he thinks, will jerk him toward death: a stain on his soul if he stays with the mistress, the death of his body if he remains with the wife. Imagination is the only way out, and he grabs for it eagerly. What a long way he is from Maggie's simultaneous knowledge of the crack and her willingness to cover it up. As for a comparison with Hester, Jerry Conant does not belong in the same room. The world of Updike's adulterers is freer than those of Hawthorne and James, but Updike also knows that increased options ironically immobilize the transgressor with the anxiety of choice. Freedom leads to despair.

NOTES

1. Tony Tanner, *Adultery in the Novel: Contract and Transgression* (Baltimore: Johns Hopkins University Press, 1979) 34.

2. Tanner 89.

3. John Updike, "Accuracy," *Picked-Up Pieces* (New York: Knopf, 1975) 17.

4. John Updike, "One Big Interview," *Picked-Up Pieces* 505.

5. Updike, "One Big Interview" 504.

6. John Updike, "The Future of the Novel," *Picked-Up Pieces* 18.

7. Updike, "The Future of the Novel" 19.

8. Updike, "The Future of the Novel" 20.

9. Updike, "The Future of the Novel" 21.

10. John Updike, "If at First You Do Succeed, Try, Try Again," *Picked-Up Pieces* 402.

11. Updike, "One Big Interview" 502, 503.

12. Updike, "One Big Interview" 509.

13. "Interview with John Updike," *First Person: Conversations on Writers and Writing*," ed. Frank Gado (Schenectady: Union College Press, 1973) 98.

14. Charles Thomas Samuels, "The Art of Fiction XLIII: John Updike," *Paris Review* 12 (1968): 102–3.

15. John Updike, *Marry Me: A Romance* (New York: Knopf, 1976) 97. Hereafter cited parenthetically.

16. John Updike, "More Love in the Western World," *Assorted Prose* (New York: Knopf, 1965) 298.

17. Samuels 100.

18. Updike, "More Love in the Western World" 299.

19. Updike, "More Love in the Western World" 299.

20. John Updike, *The Poorhouse Fair/Rabbit, Run* (New York: Modern Library, 1965) 357. This is the first revised American edition.

21. John Updike, foreword, *Too Far to Go* (New York: Fawcett Crest, 1979) 10.

22. Jane Barnes, "John Updike: A Literary Spider," *Virginia Quarterly Review* 57 (1981): 82.

23. Barnes notes that "there is a tendency in Updike's stories to inflate American boredom into French existentialist despair" (93).

24. Updike, *Rabbit, Run* 272.

25. John Updike, "Domestic Life in America," *Problems* (New York: Knopf, 1979) 165–66.

26. George W. Hunt, *John Updike and the Three Great Secret Things: Sex, Religion, and Art* (Grand Rapids: Eerdmans, 1980).

27. Updike, *Rabbit, Run* 305–6.

28. Hunt 16.

29. Samuels 85, 101.

30. For Updike's elaboration of this point, see his introduction to F. J. Sheed, ed. *Soundings in Satanism* (New York: Sheed and Ward, 1972).

31. Hunt 121.

32. John Updike, Introduction, *Soundings in Satanism* vii.

33. Updike, Introduction, *Soundings in Satanism* viii.

34. Updike, Introduction, *Soundings in Satanism* ix. See also John T. Matthews, "The Word as Scandal: Updike's *A Month of Sundays*," *Arizona Quarterly* 39 (1983):351–80.

35. Updike, Introduction, *Soundings in Satanism* x.

36. John Updike, "Faith in Search of Understanding," *Assorted Prose* 273–74.

37. John Updike, *Couples* (New York: Knopf, 1968) 17. Hereafter cited parenthetically.

38. Samuels 102.

39. Interview, *New York Times Book Review* 29 Aug. 1976:7.

40. Nathaniel Hawthorne, *The Marble Faun: Or, The Romance of Monte Beni* (Columbus: Ohio State University Press, 1968) 463.

Updike, James, and Hawthorne

eferring in *The Novel of Adultery* to such cultural anthropologists as G. P. Murdock and F. Henriques, Judith Armstrong notes that the breakup of a marriage may be called either sensible or tragic but it is rarely considered trivial. She quotes Murdock: "Marriage exists only when the economic and sexual are united in one relationship, and this combination occurs only in marriage."[1] If marriage assures order in sexual matters, the proper inheritance of property, and the perpetuation of civilized behavior, then adultery must be judged a threat to both individual security and universal stability. Violate the bedroom and society wavers. Commit adultery and the great chain of being breaks a link. Moral sanction and economic contract: society needs both to protect itself.

Interestingly, as Armstrong shows, some combination of spiritual and secular approval has always defined the development of marriage laws: "The concept of marriage had evolved considerably even before the influence of Christianity, from a 'sacral' event drawing its significance from the 'religion of the hearth' through a secularisation process which resulted in the acceptance of a partnership based on 'mutual consent,' or, alternatively and more commonly, the selection of a bride by the prospective groom's family."[2] In the Western world the spiritual sanction of marriage became increasingly important by the twelfth and thirteenth centuries when priests, following Aquinas, interpreted marriage as a sacrament that illustrated not only contract but also the sacred relationship between Christ and the Church. Thus although adultery was a grave threat, it could never be the grounds for dissolving a marriage; just as Christ is forever wed to his Church, so marriage is always eternal. The Reformed Church repudiated such a rigid accommodation of adultery, but the specter of violating religious sanction has shadowed sexual transgression for centuries.

Similarly, Armstrong notes that the fear of breaking a contract developed as property became defined in ancestral terms: "With the growth in importance of property, the reaction against adultery intensified. It was no longer a question, as in ancient times, of betrayal of the household religion; fear of the bastard as a usurper of name and land became an obsession which could join with the church to the point of vilifying the adultress but was prepared to go a great deal further in the matter of punishing her."[3] The double-barreled sanction of spiritual ceremony and secular contract threatens such transgressors as Hester Prynne, for, as Hawthorne knows, her association in the opening chapter with the Virgin and Child ironically comments on the moral and social rigidity of the Puritan mob who define Hester's freedom as an affront to their own well-being. No wonder they hope to snatch little Pearl from her. As there is no church, they insist, without Christ, and no state without a governor, so there is no family without a husband. Love, sympathy, and forgiveness are not the issues; law, confession, and punishment are. These iron-clad opinions are a long way from the idealization of women and even adultery that developed in the twelfth century with the advent of courtly love.

Today's reader readily recognizes the irony: Hawthorne celebrates parallels between Hester and the Virgin, but his fictional religious community would like to expel her from its protection; courtly love celebrates sexual activity at a time when the Church suggests that even conjugal passion may be evil, and thus inadvertently intensifies the acceptance of adultery, at least in literature. Through all the permutations in the definition of love, one notes the necessity of obstacles if passion is to thrive. Church and society may offer the official seals of approval, but marriage seems antithetical to sexual intensity. Thus the brighter the lure of adultery, the more vociferous the prohibition of moral and judicial codes. One may or may not agree with Denis de Rougemont's argument that the desire for love is the quest for obstruction and that the ultimate obstacle is death, but one understands why novelists are attracted not to serene wedlock but to the hurdles encountered on the way to the marriage ceremony and after. In the world of fiction not love itself but the

Conclusions

threats to love are eternal. One cannot imagine passion between—
or even sustained novelistic interest in—Hilda and Kenyon, the early
Maggie and Amerigo, or Angela and Piet; but Hester and Dimmesdale, Charlotte and the Prince, and Foxy and Piet are another story
indeed. The development of the sentimental novel in the eighteenth century and its variations in the nineteenth and twentieth
centuries are more or less secularized extensions of the earlier
conflation of religious fervor and courtly passion. Adultery is still
branded by the Bible, as James's Mrs. Wix memorably says, but
James, Hawthorne, Updike, and most American novelists view the
threat to be directed as much toward the stability of society as toward the salvation of souls. It is not so much the subject matter as
the emphases that vary. Hawthorne may stress the moral order,
James the social, and Updike the individual, but all three consider
sexual transgression the consummate obstacle to the peaceful marriage and thus the most attractive material for fiction.

The irony is that marriage may therefore be judged a form of punishment. As laws restrict freedom, so marriage inhibits passion. Society and religion thrive on restraint. Armstrong reminds the reader
that the Connecticut law codes of 1638–39 called for fornication to
be punished by fines, whipping, or marriage. Thus the opposition of
marriage and passion was all but codified, and American novelists
saw the irony as fascinating subject matter. Hester and Dimmesdale
cannot get married; Maggie and the Prince suffer separation within
marriage; and Rabbit, Piet, and Jerry Conant long to break out of
marriage. For all three authors, however, adultery is the cause *and*
effect of tension. Conventional marriages make dull lives and even
duller novels.

Other than *The Scarlet Letter* there are no important American
novels before the late James that dare to treat adultery as a central theme. Reading American fiction from 1850 to 1904—from
The Scarlet Letter to *The Golden Bowl*—one finds William Dean
Howells's *A Modern Instance* (1882) and *The Shadow of a Dream*
(1890) and Harold Frederic's *The Damnation of Theron Ware* (1896)
as possibilities. But in addition to being published thirty and forty
years after Hawthorne's masterpiece, and thus making Hawthorne
seem all the more prescient, these novels consider not adultery but
passion. Divorce and the decline from sexuality to frigidity are the

true subjects of *A Modern Instance*, and initiated readers know that Marcia's kissing the parlor door handle after Bartley touches the knob is a long way from Hester's letting down her hair and casting off the A. Howells was correct when he admitted that without the example of John W. De Forest's *Miss Ravenel's Conversion from Secession to Loyalty* (1867) he might not have ventured to suggest the power of sexual attraction, but the fact remains that in the early 1880s divorce was the extent of the taboos he was willing to confront. For a modern reader to understand how disturbing *A Modern Instance* was in its day, one need only remember that Robert Louis Stevenson, himself married to a divorcée, broke off his friendship with Howells for a decade because he mistakenly believed that the novel criticized divorce. Although Howells writes that following divorce Marcia's sorrow "had unsexed her," he is not interested in the complication of adultery.

The Shadow of a Dream is another matter. Taking his title from the first sentence in chapter 12 ("The Minister's Vigil") of *The Scarlet Letter*, Howells openly bows to Hawthorne in this astonishing yet little-read novel of inhibition, erotic desire, and transference of guilt. The Hester-Dimmesdale-Chillingworth triangle is repeated in the Hermia-Nevil-Faulkner entanglement, with the added—and shocking—twist that all three die. But for all his sophisticated handling of what today one would call Freudian subjects, Howells is more concerned with the *possibility* of adultery, latent homosexual attraction, and undeserved guilt than with the literal act of trangression. The minister Nevil understands that the dying Faulkner "keeps the horror, whatever it is, wholly to himself. I think if he could tell somebody he could escape it. But he can't! . . . You might suppose it was jealousy, in some suppressed form. But there never was anything of that!"[4] Perhaps Nevil is correct; perhaps he and Hermia are not attracted to one another before Faulkner dies. But with great insight Howells shows that the powers of passion and jealousy are irrational and uncontrollable and that Faulkner's loathsome dream— his union of love and death, of the marriage vow and the funeral dirge—destroys all three by the force of its suggestion.

Frederic's Reverend Theron Ware strays into a similarly structured Hawthornian world. Where Faulkner cultivates a fantastic garden straight from the pages of *The House of the Seven Gables*,

Conclusions

Ware strolls with his temptress into a forest first inhabited by Hester and Dimmesdale. Depending on the reader's inclination, the kiss that Celia offers the minister may or may not symbolize adultery, but for all the undertone of sexuality in the novel Frederic is more interested in the sin of pride and the burden of knowledge on an ignorant man. Frederic's Alice glances at Hawthorne's Hilda, just as Celia recalls Miriam, but despite the allusions to sex, adultery is not a central fact in *The Damnation of Theron Ware*.

The interesting point is that the Howells of *The Shadow of a Dream* and the Frederic of *Theron Ware* were necessary stepping stones in the development of the continuum from Hawthorne to James. Recitation of dates can be arbitrary and imply more than the accidents of time allow, but one should at least remember that following Howells's treatment of divorce in *A Modern Instance* in 1882 James added adultery as the primary cause of divorce in his 1888 novella "A London Life"; that Howells began writing *The Shadow of a Dream* in 1889 following the painful death of his daughter and his resulting confusion over psychological and physiological traumas; and that Frederic published *Theron Ware*, a novel that like *The Shadow of a Dream* looks both back to Hawthorne and forward to the late James, just before James published *What Maisie Knew*, one of his major investigations of sexual transgression and divorce, in 1897. Hawthorne and James, and to a limited extent Howells and Frederic, dared in the Victorian nineteenth century to create women who were more than what Leslie Fiedler has called "monsters of virtue." Once sexuality in women is admitted, adultery follows, and the twin restraints of religious ceremony and judicial contract are the first to feel the threat.

As the late-twentieth-century inheritor of the Hawthorne-James tradition, Updike brings his own variations, discussed in the previous chapters. But what is significant about the three authors, especially in light of Hawthorne's and Updike's religious sensibilities and James's Victorian temperament, is that not one of them condemns adultery. Hawthorne sets *The Scarlet Letter* in the distant past so as to explore sexual issues without violating either Puritan morality or the contemporary standard of strict silence in all matters physical. The same may be said for *The Marble Faun*: setting the tale in faraway Rome allows Hawthorne to offer the safety of narrative distance between the wary reader and the oblique treatment of sex outside marriage. That the sexual transgression occurs before *The Scarlet Letter* begins and that the word *adultery* is not used in the book do not detract from the status of the novel as the first great fictional account of adultery in American literature. Only the most naïve reader can ignore Hester's sensuality or can fail to see how Hawthorne surrounds the adultery with such ambiguity that the transgression seems finally to be vital, creative, and admirable. Hawthorne does not advocate unbridled sexuality, but neither does he condemn passion outside of marriage. Punishment may be an issue but not damnation. One does not forget *the* fundamental fact about Hester Prynne: She is an adulteress. All her other qualities derive from her one moment of transgression.

Contrasting Hester's passion with her accusers' lack of compassion, Hawthorne touches on the separation of flesh and spirit which he understands but hesitates fully to endorse. Rejection of the body may promise protection of the soul, but he suggests that inhibition nourishes the dichotomy of sexual transgression and spiritual atrophy. Sins of the flesh create little Pearls, while celebrations of the spirit build scaffolds. Hester's black hair reflects the darkness of the forest and is clearly an invitation to wander beyond the safety of the town; but for all her lure to the unknown, Hawthorne refuses to damn her vital mixture of red and black in favor of the Puritans' drab gray. The irony is that adultery means life to the strong; those, like Dimmesdale, who are too weak to assimilate the plunge beyond the clearing will die. None of this is expressed outright, of course, but to appreciate the impact of Hester's passion on her creator, one need only contrast her enticing yet dangerous voluptuousness with the heroine of Hawthorne's next novel: the antiseptic Phoebe of *The House of the Seven Gables*. It is as if Hawthorne looks at Hester and pulls back. Once he allows these two opposing heroines to shape the moral tones of their respective tales, he tries to have it both ways in his last two novels and offers Hesters and Phoebes in the same book: Zenobia-Priscilla, Miriam-Hilda. Thus he simultaneously invites the reader into the forest and insists on his safety in the town. Ambiguity becomes the refuge of adultery.

Even more than Hawthorne, James refuses to judge his adulterous couples. He may make them less admirable and work for their

Conclusions

defeat or discomfort, but he refrains from applying the rigors of moral censure. Not the rigidity of religious belief but the equilibrium of social discourse concerns him. Madame Merle and Gilbert Osmond of *The Portrait of a Lady* are as dishonest as Charlotte Stant and Prince Amerigo of *The Golden Bowl* are dignified, but the reader understands that both couples are wrong not because they violate the principles of moral law but because they upset the harmony of domestic affairs. James knows that without checks and balances civilized behavior falters.

Like Hawthorne, James has little interest in the particulars of adultery. More fascinated by what he calls in *The Ambassadors* the "deep, deep truth of the intimacy revealed," he probes reactions and adjustments to transgression. That such attractive women as Mme de Vionnet and Charlotte Stant freely indulge their sexuality is assumed; what matters is not so much their rewards or punishments but how their passion affects behavior. *The Golden Bowl* is his most thorough—indeed the most thorough in American literature—investigation of adultery because it dissects motivation and justification of the forbidden act. Given the sophistication of Charlotte and the Prince and their acceptance of morality as little more than "high intelligence," guilt is not an issue with them. But fear of exposure is. With an irony that is subtle even by his standards, James encourages the association of sex and knowledge and then places his transgressors in the predicament of having knowledge but remaining uncertain of what their spouses know. High intelligence leads to ignorance.

An even greater irony is that adultery can lead to creativity. Aware of *The Scarlet Letter*, in which Hester's acceptance of passion enables her to redeem the transgression that is originally caused by passion, James conceives the principal marriage in *The Golden Bowl* so that it wavers before the adultery occurs and then is strengthened because of it. Both Hawthorne and James suggest that knowledge is discovered in passion, but Hawthorne hedges when he has Hester all but forever cover her breasts and hair following the fateful liaison with Dimmesdale. James, however, details how adultery can benefit, especially when he shows Maggie admitting both the power of passion and the error of unconsciously withholding her not inconsiderable physical charms from the Prince. Adultery is based on deceit and is thus dishonest, but Maggie's ignorant fidelity is equally suspect. She can begin to create a productive marriage only after experiencing the twin shocks of sexual betrayal and her own culpability. Imposition of a moral code has little to do with her determination to shape good from bad. Surely Armstrong is correct when she writes that James's "attitude sets him apart from the other novelists in that he is indifferent to the kinds of moral imperatives they are unable to dissociate from" adultery.[5]

In "Love and Sex in Henry James," D. Singh Maini argues that James's unique power as a novelist is linked to his sexual concerns. Challenging the image of James as "that of a Victorian prude," Maini proposes to "authenticate the presence of the sexual imagination in him as a driving force almost from the start," and he suggests that James's sexual imagination turns "predatory" at the end of his career: "The sinews of his art are the sinews of sex." Needless to say, Maini begins with James's famous "obscure hurt" and proceeds, in Freudian fashion, to insist that the result of the adolescent injury was the "apotheosis of art": "The entire brood of Freudian monsters was in full cry as the novelist, retreating more and more into the sanctuaries of the imagination, fashioned 'palaces of thought' and 'pagodas' of art in gothic extravagance."[6] The monsters cry loudest as James reaches his major phase and draws on "the missed intensities of sexual experience" to create a subtle and fantastic fiction.

Given Maini's emphasis, it is interesting that he does not view James's treatment of adultery as radical. James, Maini argues, offers no stormy consummations because he writes "within the narrow confines of bourgeois marital ethics." Harmony must be maintained, even when one's sympathies are momentarily with such sexually attractive, erotically mysterious women as Charlotte Stant. But one disagrees with Maini's observation that Maggie Verver saves her marriage by evoking "compassion, sacrifice and accommodation." This opinion is relevant for the reader who believes, as Maini does, that James's sense of marriage is merely a more subtle and psychological extension of nineteenth-century American views of wedlock, best exemplified by Howells: "Heaven . . . is mirrored in each true marriage."[7] Surely such a statement applies primarily to Howells's early marriage novels. One need read only *A Modern Instance* and *The Shadow of a Dream* to understand Howells's awareness of do-

Conclusions

mestic disaster caused when passion naturally extends to jealousy, betrayal, and guilt. Popular opinion to the contrary, neither Howells nor James was innocent or prudish, at least in his fiction; and thus it is better to suggest that Maggie creates her new marriage because she learns to indulge her own passion while accommodating the adultery of her husband, and that Faulkner (*The Shadow of a Dream*) shatters his marriage because he cannot assimilate sex, guilt, and unconsciously generated fear. True marriages may mirror heaven, yet such marriages are difficult to maintain. Passion requires freedom. The value of marriage is that it signals social order, but the attraction of adultery is that it challenges the forms. James knows these truths. One does not have to join Maini and find "grisly and shaggy creatures of the Freudian menagerie" in the late James to appreciate the stunning power of sexuality in *The Golden Bowl*. [8]

James shows that ethics have little to do with the creation or destruction of marital order. Maggie's determination to fight for the Prince enables her to free her own passion; in effect she fights sex with sex. Acknowledging the ground-breaking treatment of adultery by James and Hawthorne, Updike follows them in refusing to judge unsanctioned love from the pinnacle of an arbitrary moral code. Although more Puritan-haunted than James and thus more religiously oriented, he too shows that ethical considerations are not of the moment. One variation he offers is that of uniting James's concern with social harmony and Hawthorne's interest in religious imperatives. But where James probes the social and Hawthorne the moral, Updike investigates the individual who is stranded on Karl Barth's border between the conceivable and the inconceivable. Sexual transgression extends both physical and spiritual horizons for Updike's adulterers, and they find themselves questing for the promise that they will never die. It is interesting, too, that while his predecessors focus on women, Updike writes largely about men. Women offer the paradox of freedom and entrapment, and his male adulterers simultaneously long to fall and fear the plunge. When he does detail the female's point of view, as with Ruth in *Marry Me*, he adapts James's example of the wife struggling for her wandering husband and reveals that Ruth also engages in adultery. Adultery is similarly creative, for her self-definition is the result. Ruth, Rabbit, Piet, Jerry Conant, and the Reverend Tom Marshfield can know themselves only if they stray beyond the clearing. When they do, they find Hester and Miriam and the Prince, and, more important, the Hawthorne and James who originally placed them there.

NOTES

1. Judith Armstrong, *The Novel of Adultery* (London: Macmillan, 1976) 2.
2. Armstrong 3.
3. Armstrong 6.
4. William Dean Howells, *The Shadow of a Dream* and *An Imperative Duty* (Bloomington: Indiana University Press, 1970) 41.
5. Armstrong 145.
6. D. Singh Maini, "Love and Sex in Henry James," in *Proceedings of a Symposium on American Literature* (Poznán, Poland: Uniwersytet im. Adama Micklewicza w Poznaniu, 1979) 108, 109, 110.
7. Maini 114.
8. Maini 116.

Index

136

Index